10

MINUTE
GUIDE TO
Excel 5

Joe Kraynak

**alpha
books**

A Division of Macmillan Computer Publishing USA
A Prentice Hall Macmillan Company
201 West 103rd Street, Indianapolis, Indiana 46290 USA

To my kids, Nick and Ali, for making me laugh.

©1993 by Alpha Books

International Standard Book Number: 1-56761-321-7
Library of Congress Catalog Card Number: 93-72160

96 95   8 7 6 5

Interpretation of the printing code: the rightmost double-digit number is the year of the book's first printing; the rightmost single-digit number is the number of the book's printing. For example, a printing code of 93-1 shows that this copy of the book was printed during the first printing of the book in 1993.

Publisher: *Marie Butler-Knight*

Product Development Manager: *Faithe Wempen*

Managing Editor: *Elizabeth Keaffaber*

Development Editor: *Seta Frantz*

Production Editor: *Linda Hawkins*

Manuscript Editor: *San Dee Phillips*

Cover Design: *Dan Armstrong*

Designer: *Roger Morgan*

Indexer: *Jeanne Clark*

Production Team: *Gary Adair, Kate Bodenmiller, Brad Chinn, Kim Cofer, Tim Cox, Meshell Dinn, Stephanie Gregory, Diana Bigham-Griffin, Jenny Kucera, Beth Rago, Marc Shecter, Greg Simsic*

Special thanks to Kelly Oliver for ensuring the technical accuracy of this book.

Screen reproductions in this book were created by means of the program Collage Plus from Inner Media, Inc., Hollis, NH.

Contents

Introduction

Perhaps you walked into work this morning and found Excel 5 on your desk. A note is stuck to the box: "We need a budget report for the upcoming meeting. See what you can do."

Now What?

You could wade through the manuals that came with the program to find out how to perform a specific task, but that may take a while, and it may tell you more than you want to know. You need a practical guide, one that will tell you exactly how to create and print the worksheets, reports, and graphs you need for the meeting.

Welcome to the 10 Minute Guide to Excel 5

Because most people don't have the luxury of sitting down uninterrupted for hours at a time to learn Excel, this *10 Minute Guide* does not attempt to teach *everything* about the program. Instead, it focuses on the most often-used features. Each feature is covered in a single self-contained lesson, which is designed to take 10 minutes or less to complete.

The *10 Minute Guide* teaches you about the program without relying on technical jargon. With straightforward, easy-to-follow explanations and numbered lists that tell you what keys to press and what options to select, the *10 Minute Guide to Excel* 5 makes learning the program quick and easy.

Who Should Use the 10 Minute Guide to Excel 5?

The *10 Minute Guide to Excel 5* is for anyone who

- Needs to learn Excel 5 quickly.

- Feels overwhelmed or intimidated by the complexity of Excel 5.

- Wants to find out quickly whether Excel 5 will meet his or her computing needs.

- Wants a clear, concise guide to the most important features of Excel 5.

How to Use This Book

The *10 Minute Guide to Excel 5* consists of a series of lessons ranging from basic startup to a few more advanced features. If this is your first encounter with Excel 5, you should probably work through lessons 1 to 12 in order. These lessons lead you through the process of creating, editing, and printing a spreadsheet. Subsequent lessons tell you how to use the more advanced features to customize your spreadsheet; use your spreadsheet as a database; create, enhance, and print graphs; and generate reports.

If Excel 5 has not been installed on your computer, consult the inside front cover for installation steps. If this is your first encounter with Microsoft Windows, turn to Appendix A, "Microsoft Windows Primer," at the end of this book for help.

Icons and Conventions Used in This Book

The following icons have been added throughout the book to help you find your way around:

Timesaver Tip icons offer shortcuts and hints for using the program efficiently.

Plain English icons define new terms.

Panic Button icons appear where new users often run into trouble.

In addition, Excel version 5 icons help you identify features that are new to Microsoft Excel 5. You can quickly take advantage of the latest timesaving features of Excel.

The following conventions have been used to clarify the steps you must perform:

On-screen text	Any text that appears on-screen is shown in **bold**.
What you type	The information you type appears in **bold and in color**.
Menu names	The names of menus, commands, buttons, and dialog boxes are shown with the first letter capitalized for easy recognition.
Option selections	In any Windows application, you can select an option by using your mouse or by typing the underlined letter in the option's name. In this book, the bold letter corresponds to the underlined letter you see on-screen.

Key+Key Combinations	In many cases, you must press a two-key combination in order to enter a command. For example, "Press Alt+X." In such cases, hold down the first key while pressing the second key.

For Further Reference . . .

If you want a more detailed guide to using Microsoft Excel, we suggest the following books from Alpha Books:

The Complete Idiot's Guide to Excel 5 by Ricardo Birmele.

The First Book of Excel 5 by Galen Grimes.

The Excel 5 HyperGuide by Howard Hansen.

If you learn better by having someone show you how it's done, try *Show Me Excel 5* by Seta Frantz.

If you are looking for a comprehensive quick reference to Excel 5, try *One Minute Reference: Excel 5*.

Trademarks

All terms mentioned in this book that are known to be trademarks or service marks are listed below. In addition, terms suspected of being trademarks or service marks have been appropriately capitalized. Alpha Books cannot attest to the accuracy of this information. Use of a term in this book should not be regarded as affecting the validity of any trademark or service mark.

MS-DOS, Windows, Excel, and Toolbar are trademarks of Microsoft Corporation.

Lesson

Starting and Exiting Excel

In this lesson, you'll learn how to start and end a typical Excel work session and how to get on-line help.

Starting Excel

To use Excel, you must master some basic techniques in Microsoft Windows, including opening program group windows, running applications, dragging, and scrolling. If these terms are unfamiliar to you, refer to the Windows Primer at the back of this book before moving on.

After you installed Excel (see the inside front cover of this book), the installation program returned you to the Program Manager and displayed the Microsoft Office program group window as shown in Figure 1.1. This window contains the icon you use to start Excel. To start Excel, follow these steps:

- Double-click on the Microsoft Excel icon.

OR

- Use the arrow keys to highlight the icon, and press Enter.

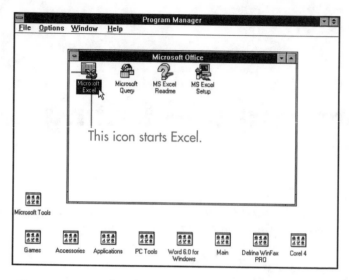

Figure 1.1   Select the Microsoft Excel application icon to run the program.

The Excel opening screen appears (see Figure 1.2) with a blank workbook labeled Book1. Excel is now ready for you to begin creating your workbook.

> **Workbook**   Excel files are called *workbooks*. Each workbook consists of 16 worksheets. Each worksheet consists of columns and rows that intersect to form boxes called *cells* into which you enter text. The tabs at the bottom of the workbook let you flip through the worksheets.

You will perform most operations in Excel using the menu bar, at the top of the screen, and the Standard toolbar, just below it. You'll learn about the various operations in later lessons.

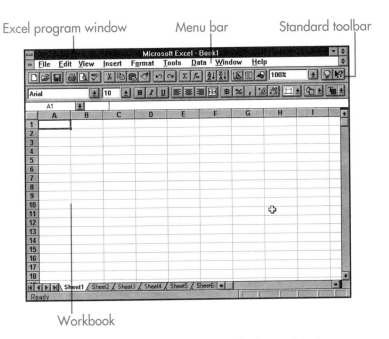

Excel program window   Menu bar   Standard toolbar

Workbook

Figure 1.2   Excel's opening screen displays a blank workbook.

Getting Help

You can get help in Excel for Windows in three different ways:

> **Pull down the Help menu.** Pull down the Help menu for various help options. You can then select Contents (for groups of help topics), **S**earch for Help on (to search for a specific topic), **I**ndex (for a list of help topics from A to Z), **Q**uick Preview (for a brief tour of Excel), **E**xamples and Demos (to see how to perform various tasks), **L**otus 1-2-3 or **M**ultiplan (for specific details on how to make the transition from

those programs), **Technical Support** (for information on what to do when all else fails), or **About Microsoft Excel** (for licensing and system information).

Press F1. Press the F1 key to view various groups of Help topics. Pressing F1 is equivalent to choosing Contents from the Help menu. If you press F1 when a menu item or dialog box is displayed, you get help for that item or box. If you press F1 when a Help window is displayed, you get information about how to use the Help system.

Click on the Help button. The Help button is in the Standard toolbar; it's the button that has the arrow and the question mark on it. When you click on the Help button, the mouse pointer turns into an arrow with a question mark. Click on any item or part of the screen with which you need help, and Excel displays help for that item or screen area. Double-click on the Help button to search for a Help topic.

Getting Around in a Help Window

When you select a Help option, Excel displays a Help window like the one in Figure 1.3. You can resize the window as you can resize any window. Use the scroll bar to view any information that does not fit in the window.

Most Help windows contain terms or topics that are underlined with a solid or dotted line. These are called *jumps*. If you click on a term that's dotted underlined, Excel displays a pop-up text box that provides a bit more information about the term. Click on a term or topic that is solid underlined, Excel displays help for the selected item or kicks you out to a How To Help screen.

Help window

Use these buttons to move
around in the Help system.

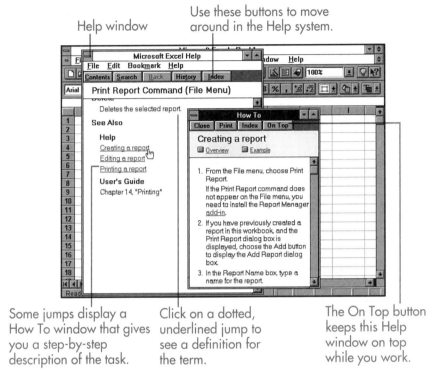

Some jumps display a
How To window that gives
you a step-by-step
description of the task.

Click on a dotted,
underlined jump to
see a definition for
the term.

The On Top button
keeps this Help
window on top
while you work.

Figure 1.3 When you choose a Help option, a Help window
appears, covering a portion of the screen.

To move around in the Help system, click on the
following buttons at the top of the Help window, or hold
down the Alt key and press the underlined letter in the
button's name:

Contents displays groups of Help topics.

Search allows you to search for a topic by typing the
name of the topic. As you type, the cursor highlights
the name of the topic that matches your entry. Keep
typing until the desired topic is displayed, and then
press Enter.

Back displays the previous Help screen.

History displays a list of recently accessed Help topics. This is useful if you commonly view the same Help topic.

Index displays a comprehensive list of Help topics in alphabetical order.

Glossary (not always displayed) provides a list of terms for which you can get definitions.

To exit Help, perform any of the following steps:

* Press Alt+F4, or double-click on the Control-menu box in the upper left corner of the Help window.

* Press Alt+F, or click on File in the Help window, and select Exit (or press X).

* Click on the Minimize button in the upper right corner of the Help window to shrink the window down to an icon. This doesn't exit the Help system, it just moves it out of the way. To get the help window back, press Ctrl+Esc, and double-click on its name.

Discovering More with the TipWizard

Excel 5.0 offers a new feature called the TipWizard that provides information about how to fully exploit the power of Excel. The TipWizard looks at what you are currently doing and provides tips on how to do it faster. To turn the TipWizard on or off, click on the TipWizard button on the Standard toolbar, as shown in Figure 1.4.

Exiting Excel

To exit Excel and return to the Program Manager, follow these steps:

Standard toolbar

Use these buttons to move to the next or previous tip.

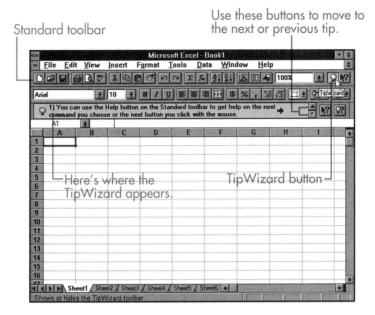

Here's where the TipWizard appears.

TipWizard button

Figure 1.4 The TipWizard offers timesaving advice.

1. Press Alt+F or click on File on the menu bar.

2. Press X, or click on Exit.

If you changed the workbook in any way without saving the file, Excel will display a prompt asking if you want to save the file before exiting. Select the desired option.

> **Quick Exit** For a quick exit, press Alt+F4, or double-click on the Control-menu box in the upper left corner of the Excel window.

In this lesson, you learned how to enter and exit Excel and get on-line help. In the next lesson, you'll learn about the Excel workbook window.

Lesson

Moving Around in the Excel Window

In this lesson, you'll learn the basics of moving around in the Excel window and in the workbook window.

Navigating the Excel Window

As you can see in Figure 2.1, the Excel window contains several elements that allow you to enter commands and data:

Menu bar   Displays the names of the available pull-down menus. When you select a menu, it drops down over a portion of the screen, presenting you with a list of options.

Toolbars   Contain several icons, buttons, and drop-down lists that give you quick access to often-used commands and features.

Formula bar   To enter information in a cell, you select the cell and type the information in the formula bar. When you press Enter, the information is inserted in the selected cell.

Workbook window   Contains the workbook where you will enter the data and formulas that make up your workbook.

Status bar   Displays information about the current activity, including help information and keyboard and program modes.

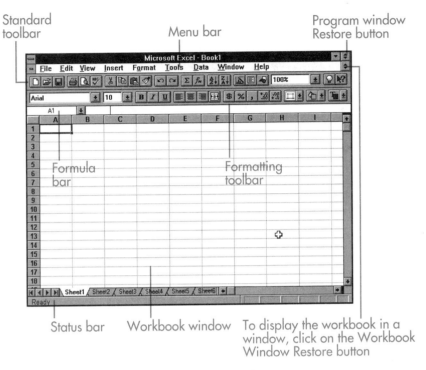

Figure 2.1 Elements of the Excel window.

Sizing Windows When you run Excel, it starts in full-screen mode. You can resize the window at any time. Click on the Restore button in the upper right corner of the window and then drag the window border to size the window.

Navigating the Workbook Window

Inside the Excel program window is a workbook window with the current worksheet in front. In this window, you will enter the labels, values, and formulas that make up each worksheet. Figure 2.2 illustrates the various parts of the workbook. Table 2.1 describes the parts.

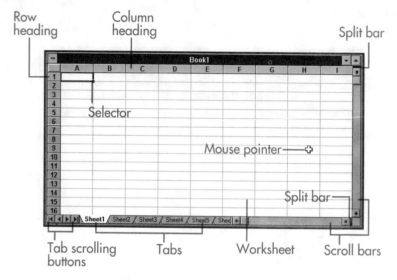

Figure 2.2   Elements of the workbook window.

Table 2.1   Workbook window items.

Item	Function
Tabs	A workbook consists of 16 worksheets. You can use the tabs to flip worksheets.
Tab scrolling buttons	Allow you to scroll through the worksheets in the workbook.
Scroll bars	Allow you to view a section of the current worksheet that is not displayed.
Column heading	Identifies the column by letters.
Row heading	Identifies the row by numbers.
Selector	Outline that indicates the active cell.
Split bars	Let you split the workbook window into two panes to view different portions of the same worksheet.

What's a Cell? Each page in a workbook is a separate worksheet. Each worksheet contains a grid consisting of alphabetized columns and numbered rows. When a row and column intersect, they form a box called a *cell*. Each cell has an *address* that consists of the column letter and row number (A1, B3, C4, and so on). You will enter data and formulas in the cells to form your worksheets. You will learn more about cells in Lesson 5.

Flipping Worksheets

Because each workbook consists of 16 worksheets, you need a way to move from worksheet to worksheet. If you are using the keyboard, you can flip worksheets by pressing Ctrl+PgDn and Ctrl+PgUp.

If you are using the mouse, there are easier ways to flip worksheets. If a tab is shown for the worksheet you want to move to, click on the tab for that worksheet (see Figure 2.3). If the tab is not shown, use the scroll buttons to bring the tab into view, and then click on the tab.

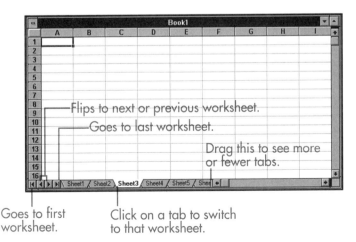

Figure 2.3 You can move from worksheet to worksheet with tabs.

Moving on a Worksheet

Once the worksheet you want to work on is displayed, you need some way of moving to the various cells on the worksheet. Keep in mind that the part of the worksheet displayed on-screen is only a small part of the worksheet, as illustrated in Figure 2.4.

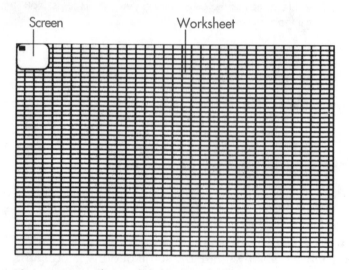

Figure 2.4 The worksheet area displayed on-screen is a small portion of the worksheet.

To move around the worksheet with your keyboard, use the keys as described in Table 2.2.

Table 2.2 Moving around a worksheet with the keyboard.

Press	To Move
←→↑↓	One cell in the direction of the arrow.
Ctrl+↑ or Ctrl+↓	To the top or bottom of a data region (an area of the worksheet that contains data).

Press	To Move
Ctrl+← or Ctrl+→	To the leftmost or rightmost cell in a data region.
PgUp	Up one screen.
PgDn	Down one screen.
Home	Leftmost cell in a row.
Ctrl+Home	Upper left corner of a worksheet.
Ctrl+End	Lower left corner of a worksheet.
End+↑, End+↓, End+←, End+→	If the active cell is blank, moves to the next blank cell in the direction of the arrow. If the active cell contains an entry, moves in the direction of the arrow to the next cell that has an entry.
End+Enter	Last column in row.

If you have a mouse, moving on a worksheet is easier. Use the scroll bars to scroll to the area of the screen that contains the cell you want to work with. Then, click on the cell. To use the scroll bars:

- Click once on a scroll arrow at the end of the scroll bar to scroll incrementally in the direction of the arrow. Hold down the mouse button to scroll continuously.

- Drag the scroll box inside the scroll bar to the area of the worksheet you want to view. For example, to move to the middle of the worksheet, drag the scroll box to the middle of the scroll bar.

- Click once inside the scroll bar, on either side of the scroll box, to move the view one screenful at a time.

F5 (Goto) for Quick Movement! To move to a specific cell on a worksheet, pull down the Edit menu and select Go To, or press F5. Type the cell's address in the Reference text box; the address consists of the column letter and row number that define the location of the cell, for example m25. To go to a cell on a specific page, type the page name, an exclamation point, and the cell address (for example, sheet3!m25. Click on the OK button.

Splitting a Worksheet

Because a worksheet can be so large, you may want to view different parts of the worksheet at the same time. To do this, you need to split the workbook window into panes. Here's how you work with panes:

- To split a workbook window, drag one of the split bars, as shown in Figure 2.5.

- To switch from one pane to the other, click in the pane you want to work with.

- To close a pane, drag the split bar to the right side or bottom of the window, and release the mouse button.

- To keep the top or left pane from scrolling, open the Window menu, and choose Freeze Panes. With the panes frozen, as you scroll in the bottom or right pane, the view in the other pane stays put.

- To free the panes, open the Window menu, and choose Unfreeze Panes.

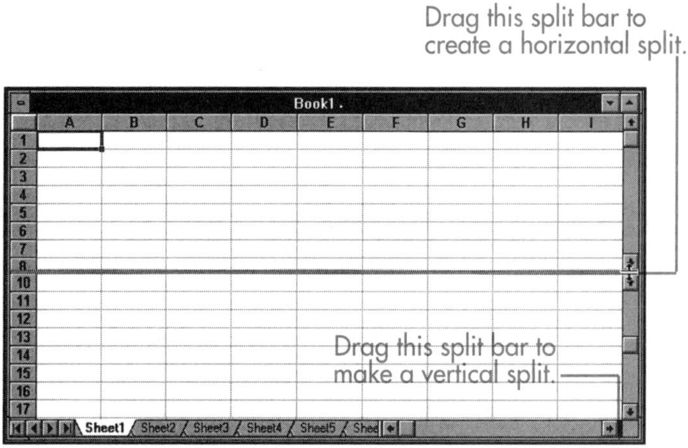

Drag this split bar to
create a horizontal split.

Drag this split bar to
make a vertical split.

Figure 2.5   Drag one of the split bars to divide the window
into two panes.

In this lesson, you learned how to move around in the
Excel window and move around in workbooks. In the next
lesson, you will learn how to use Excel's toolbars.

Lesson

Using Excel's Toolbars

In this lesson, you will learn how to use Excel's toolbars to save time when you work. You will also learn how to arrange them for maximum performance.

Using the Standard Toolbar

Unless you tell it otherwise, Excel displays the Standard and Formatting toolbars as shown in Figure 3.1. To select a tool from a toolbar, click on that tool.

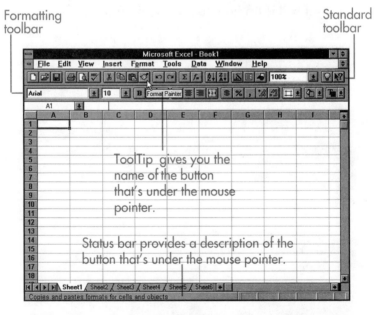

Figure 3.1 The Standard and Formatting toolbars contain buttons for the most commonly used features.

What Is a Toolbar? An Excel toolbar is a collection of tools or shortcut icons displayed in a long bar that can be moved and reshaped to suit your needs.

Learning More About Toolbar Buttons

Although I could give you a list of all the tools in the Standard toolbar and in all the other toolbars (over 270 buttons in all), here are some better ways to learn about the buttons for yourself:

To see the name of a button, move the mouse pointer over the button. Excel displays a *ToolTip* that provides the name of the button, as shown in Figure 3.1.

* To learn what a button does, move the mouse pointer over the button and look at the status bar (bottom of the screen). If the button is available for the task you are currently performing, Excel displays a description of what the button does.

* To learn more about a button, click on the Help button in the Standard toolbar (the button with the arrow and question mark), and then click on the button for which you want more information.

Turning Toolbars On or Off

Excel initially displays the Standard and Formatting toolbars. If you never use one of these toolbars, you can turn one or both of them off to free up some screen space. In addition, you can turn on other toolbars. You can turn a toolbar on or off by using the View Toolbars option or the shortcut menu.

To use the **View Toolbars** option:

1. Open the View menu, and choose Toolbars. The Toolbars dialog box appears, as shown in Figure 3.2.

2. Select the toolbar(s) you would like to hide or display. An **X** in the toolbar's check box means the bar will be displayed.

3. Click on the OK button.

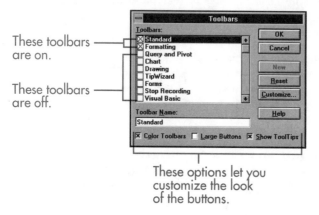

These toolbars are on.

These toolbars are off.

These options let you customize the look of the buttons.

Figure 3.2   Use the Toolbars dialog box to control the toolbars.

To use the shortcut menu to hide or display a toolbar:

1. Move the mouse pointer anywhere inside any toolbar.

2. Click on the right mouse button. The Toolbars shortcut menu appears.

3. Click on a toolbar name to turn it on if it is off or off if it is on. Excel places a check mark next to the name of a displayed toolbar.

Is It Getting Crowded in Here? Display
only the toolbars you need. Toolbars take up
screen space and memory.

Moving Toolbars

After you have displayed the toolbars you need, you may
position them in your work area where they are most convenient. Figure 3.3 shows an Excel screen with three toolbars
in various positions on the screen.

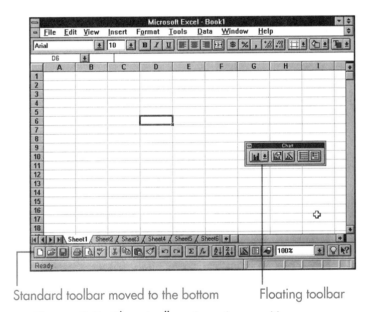

Standard toolbar moved to the bottom   Floating toolbar

Figure 3.3 Three toolbars in various positions.

Here's what you do to move a toolbar:

1. Move the mouse pointer over a buttonless part of
   the toolbar.

2. Hold down the mouse button, and drag the toolbar
   where you want it:

• Drag the toolbar to a toolbar dock. There are four toolbar docks: between the formula bar and menu bar, on the left and right sides of the Excel window, and at the bottom of the Excel window. If a toolbar contains a drop-down list, you cannot drag it to a left or right toolbar dock.

Floating Toolbar A floating toolbar acts just like a window. You can drag its title bar to move it or drag a border to size it. If you drag a floating toolbar to the top or bottom of the screen, it turns back into a horizontal toolbar.

Docking a Floating Toolbar To quickly move a floating toolbar to the top of the screen, double-click on its title bar.

Customizing the Toolbars

If Excel's toolbars provide too few (or too many) options for you, you can create your own toolbars or customize existing toolbars. To make your own toolbar, do this:

1. Open the View menu, and choose Toolbars.

2. In the Toolbar Name text box, type the name you want to give your toolbar.

3. Click on the New button. Excel creates a new floating toolbar and displays the Customize dialog box, so you can start adding buttons to your bar.

4. Drag the desired buttons onto the toolbar, as shown in Figure 3.4. For more details, continue on to the next set of steps.

5. Select Close.

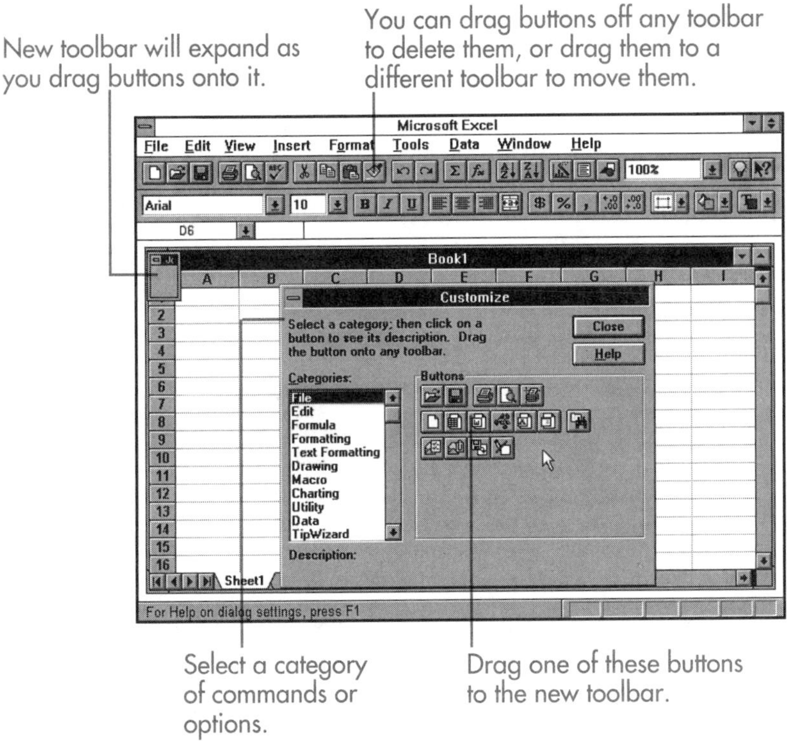

New toolbar will expand as you drag buttons onto it.

You can drag buttons off any toolbar to delete them, or drag them to a different toolbar to move them.

Select a category of commands or options.

Drag one of these buttons to the new toolbar.

Figure 3.4 Drag buttons from the Customize dialog box to the new toolbar.

You can add or remove buttons from any toolbar (Excel's or your own) by performing the following steps:

1. Do one of the following:

- Right-click on the toolbar you want to customize, and choose Customize.

- Open the View menu, and choose Toolbars. Highlight the name of the toolbar you want to customize, and choose Customize.

2. To remove a button from any toolbar, drag it off the toolbar.

3. Select the type of item you want to add from the Categories list. For example, you can add buttons for file commands, formulas, formatting, or macros. You'll see a collection of buttons. Click on a button to view its description.

4. Drag the desired button(s) onto a toolbar (any toolbar that's displayed).

5. Click on the Close button when you're done.

> **Resetting Toolbars** If you mess up one of Excel's toolbars, you can return to the factory settings at a click of the button. Choose View Toolbars, highlight the name of the toolbar you want to reset, and then click on the Reset button.

In this lesson, you learned how to use Excel's toolbars and customize toolbars for your own unique needs. In the next lesson, you will learn how to work with Excel's workbooks.

Lesson

Working with Workbook Files

In this lesson you will learn how to save, close, and open workbook files, and how to create new workbooks.

Saving a Workbook

Whatever you type into a workbook is stored only in your computer's memory. If you exit Excel, that data will be lost, so it is important to save your workbook files to disk regularly.

The first time you save a workbook to disk, you have to name it. Here's how you do it:

1. Pull down the File menu, and select Save, or click on the Save button in the Standard toolbar. The Save As dialog box appears as shown in Figure 4.1.

2. Type a name for the workbook in the File Name text box. You may use any combination of letters or numbers up to eight characters (no spaces), such as 1994BDGT. Excel automatically adds .XLS to the file name as an extension. The full file name is then 1994BDGT.XLS.

3. To save the file on a different drive, click on the arrow to the right of the Drives drop-down list, and click on the desired drive.

4. To save the file to a different directory, double-click on that directory in the **D**irectories list box. (You can move up the directory tree by double-clicking on the directory name or drive letter at the top of the tree.)

5. Click on OK, or press Enter.

Type a name for the workbook.

Select a directory.

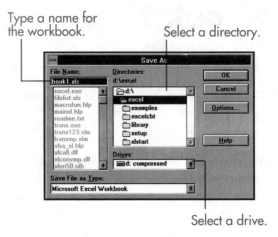

Select a drive.

Figure 4.1 The Save As dialog box.

Default Directory You can set up a default directory where Excel will save all your workbook files. Open the Tools menu, and select Options. Click on the General tab. Click inside the **D**efault File Location text box, and type a complete path to the drive and directory you want to use (the directory must be an existing one). Select OK.

To save a file you have already saved (and named), simply click on the Save button, or press Ctrl+S. Or open the File menu, and select Save. Excel automatically saves the

workbook (including any changes you entered) without
displaying the Save As dialog box.

Saving a File Under a New Name

Sometimes, you may want to change a workbook without
changing the original workbook, or you may want to create a
new workbook by modifying an existing one. You can do
this by saving the workbook under another name or in
another directory. Here's how you do it:

1. Pull down the File menu, and select Save As. You
   get the Save As dialog box, just as if you were saving
   the workbook for the first time.

2. To save the workbook under a new name, type the
   new file name over the existing name in the File
   Name text box.

3. To save the file on a different drive or directory,
   select the drive letter from the Drives list and the
   directory from the Directories list.

4. To save the file in a different format (for example,
   Lotus 1-2-3 or Quattro Pro), click on the arrow to
   the right of the Save File as Type drop-down list,
   and select the desired format.

5. Click on OK, or press Enter.

> **Backup Files**   You can have Excel create a
> backup copy of each workbook file you save.
> That way, if anything happens to the original file,
> you can use the backup copy. Backup copies have
> the same file name as the original workbook but include
> the extension .BAK. To turn the backup feature on, click
> on the Options button in the Save As dialog box, select
> Always Create Backup, and click on OK.

Creating a New Workbook

You can create a new workbook by modifying an existing
one or by opening a blank workbook and starting from
scratch. Here's how you open a blank workbook:

1. Pull down the File menu, and select New or press
Ctrl+N. The New dialog box, shown in Figure 4.2,
may or may not appear, depending on whether the
Slideshow feature is installed.

2. Choose Workbook.

3. Click on OK, or press Enter. A new workbook
opens on-screen with a default name in the title bar.
Excel numbers the files sequentially. For example, if
you already have Book1 open, the Workbook title
bar will read **Book2**.

Figure 4.2 The New dialog box.

Instant Workbook   You can bypass the New
dialog box (assuming you get it when you select
File New), by simply clicking on the New
Workbook button (the leftmost button) in the
Standard toolbar. Excel opens a new workbook window
without prompting you.

Closing Workbooks

Closing a workbook removes its workbook window from the screen. To close a workbook, do this:

1. Make the window you want to close active.

2. Pull down the File menu, and select Close. If you have not yet saved the Workbook, you will be prompted to do so.

> **In a Hurry?** To quickly close a workbook, double-click on the Control-menu box located in the upper left corner or press Ctrl+F4. If you have more than one workbook open, you can close all of them by holding down the Shift key while selecting File Close All.

Opening an Existing Workbook

If you close a workbook and you want to use the workbook later, you must open it. Here's how you do it:

1. Pull down the File menu, and select Open, or click on the Open button in the Standard toolbar (it's the button that looks like a manila folder). The Open dialog box appears, as shown in Figure 4.3.

2. If the file is not on the current drive, click on the arrow to the right of the Drives list box, and select the correct drive.

3. If the file is not in the current directory, select the correct directory from the **D**irectories list box.

4. Do one of the following:

- Choose the file you want to open from the File Name list.

- Type the name of the file in the File **Name** box. As you type, Excel highlights the first file name in the list that matches your entry (this is a quick way to move through the list).

5. Click on OK, or press Enter.

Type the file name, or select the file from the list.

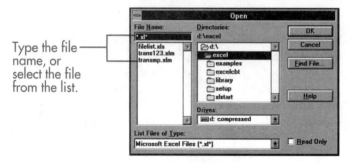

Figure 4.3 The Open dialog box.

Recently Used Workbooks Near the bottom of the File menu is a list of the most recently opened workbooks. You can quickly open the workbook by selecting it from the File menu.

Searching for Misplaced Files

If you forgot where you saved a file, Excel can help you with its new Find File feature. Here's what you do to have Excel hunt for a file:

1. Open the File menu, and select Find File, or click on the Find File button in the Open dialog box. You'll get the Search dialog box, as shown in Figure 4.4.

Wrong dialog box? If you get the Find File dialog box instead of the Search dialog box, click on the Search button at the bottom of the Find File dialog box.

2. In the File Name text box, type the name of the file you are looking for. You can use wild-card characters in place of characters you can't remember. Use an asterisk (*) in place of a group of characters, or use a question mark (?) in place of a single character. For example, *.xls finds all files with the extension .xls, and sales??.xls finds all files, such as SALES01.XLS, SALES02.XLS, and so on.

3. In the Location text box, type the drive and directory you want to search. For example, if you type c:\, Excel will search the entire C drive. Type c:\excel, and Excel searches only the EXCEL directory on drive C.

4. To have Excel search all subdirectories of the drive you specify, place an **X** in the Include Subdirectories check box.

5. Don't worry about the Clear option. It clears out anything you may have typed in the File Name and Location text boxes.

6. Click on the OK button. Excel finds the files that match the search instructions you entered, and displays them in the Find File dialog box.

7. Look through the list, highlight the file you want, and click on the Open button.

Moving Among Open Workbooks

Sometimes, you may have more than one workbook open at a time. There are several ways to move among open workbooks:

- If part of the desired workbook window is visible, click on it.

- Open the Window menu, and select the name of the workbook you want to go to.

- Press Ctrl+F6 to move from one workbook window to another.

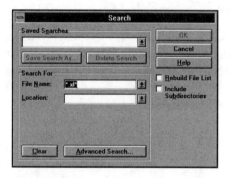

Figure 4.4 The Search dialog box asks you to specify what you want to search for.

The Active Window   If you have more than one workbook open, only one of them is considered active—the workbook where the cell selector is located. The title bar of the active workbook will be darker than the title bars of other open workbooks.

In this lesson, you learned how to save, close, and open workbooks. The next lesson teaches you how to work with the worksheets in a workbook.

Lesson

Working with Worksheets

This lesson teaches you how to add worksheets to and delete worksheets from workbooks. You will also learn how to copy, move, and rename worksheets.

By default, each workbook consists of 16 worksheet pages that are separated by tabs. You can insert new worksheet pages or delete worksheet pages as desired. You can also copy and move worksheets within a workbook or from one workbook to another.

Selecting Worksheets

Before we get into the details of inserting, deleting, and copying worksheets, you should know how to select one or more worksheets. Here's what you need to know:

- To select a single worksheet, click on its tab.

- To select several neighboring worksheets, click on the first worksheet in the group, and then hold down the Shift key while clicking on the last worksheet.

- To select several non-neighboring worksheets, hold down the Ctrl key while clicking on each worksheet.

- If you select two or more worksheets, they remain selected until you ungroup them. To ungroup worksheets, do one of the following: right-click on one of the selected worksheets, and choose Ungroup Sheets; hold down the Shift key while clicking on the active tab; or click on any tab outside the group.

Inserting Worksheets

To insert a new worksheet in a workbook, perform the following steps:

1. Select the worksheet before which you want the new worksheet inserted. For example, if you select Sheet4, the new worksheet (Sheet17) will be inserted before Sheet4.

2. Open the Insert menu.

3. Select Worksheet. Excel inserts the new worksheet, as shown in Figure 5.1.

> Shorcut Menu   A faster way to work with worksheets is to right-click on the worksheet tab. This brings up a shortcut menu that lets you insert, delete, move, copy, or rename worksheets.

Deleting Worksheets

If you plan on using only one worksheet, you can remove the 15 other worksheets to free up memory and system resources. Here's how you remove a worksheet:

1. Select the worksheet(s) you want to delete.

2. Open the Edit menu.

3. Click on Delete Sheet. A dialog box appears, asking you to confirm the deletion.

4. Click on the OK button. The worksheets are deleted.

Worksheet inserted
before Sheet 4.

Figure 5.1 Excel inserts the new worksheet before the current worksheet.

Moving and Copying Worksheets

You can move or copy worksheets within a workbook or from one workbook to another. Here's how:

1. Select the worksheet(s) you want to move or copy.

2. Open the Edit menu, and choose Move or Copy Sheet. The Move or Copy dialog box appears, as shown in Figure 5.2.

3. To move the worksheet(s) to a different workbook, select the workbook's name from the **T**o Book drop-down list.

4. Choose the worksheet before which you want the selected worksheet(s) moved from the **B**efore Sheet list box.

5. To copy the selected worksheet(s) (rather than move), select **C**reate a Copy to put an **X** in the check box.

6. Select OK. The selected worksheet(s) are copied or moved, as specified.

To move the selected worksheet(s) to a different workbook, select the workbook.

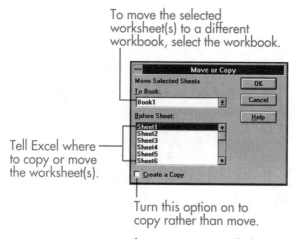

Tell Excel where to copy or move the worksheet(s).

Turn this option on to copy rather than move.

Figure 5.2 The Move or Copy dialog box asks you to specify your preferences.

Drag and Drop An easier way to copy or move worksheets is to use the Drag & Drop feature. First, select the worksheet tab(s) you want to copy or move. Move the mouse pointer over one of the selected tabs, and drag the tab where you want it moved. To copy the worksheet, hold down the Ctrl key while dragging. When you release the mouse button, the worksheet is copied or moved.

Changing the Worksheet Tab Names

By default, all worksheets are named Sheet and are numbered starting with the number 1. You can change the names that appear on the tabs. Here's how you do it:

1. Select the worksheet whose name you want to change.

2. Open the Format menu, select Sheet and then **R**ename. Or double-click on the worksheet's tab. Excel shows you the Rename Sheet dialog box, as shown in Figure 5.3.

3. Type a new name for the worksheet, and click on the OK button.

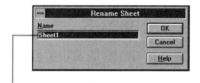

Type a new name for the worksheet.

Figure 5.3   Excel lets you give your worksheets more meaningful names.

In this lesson, you learned how to insert, delete, move, copy, and rename worksheets. In the next lesson, you will learn how to enter data into the cells in a worksheet.

Lesson

Entering and Editing Data

In this lesson, you will learn how to enter different types of data in an Excel worksheet.

Types of Data

To create a worksheet that does something, you must enter data into the cells that make up the worksheet. There are many types of data that you can enter, including:

- Text
- Numbers
- Dates
- Times
- Formulas and functions

Entering Text

You can enter any combination of letters and numbers as text. Text is automatically left-aligned in a cell.

To enter text into a cell:

1. Select the cell into which you want to enter text.

2. Type the text. As you type, your text appears in the cell and in the formula bar, as shown in Figure 6.1.

3. Click on the Enter button on the formula bar (the button with the check mark on it), or press Enter.

Enter button

Function Wizard button (you'll learn about it in Lesson 11)

Cancel button

Figure 6.1   Data that you enter also appears on the formula bar.

Bail out!   To cancel an entry before you are done, click on the Cancel button (the button with the X on it), or press Esc.

Number Text   You may want to enter a number as text (for example, a ZIP code). Precede your entry with a single quotation mark ('), as in '46220. The single quotation mark is an alignment prefix that tells Excel to treat the following characters as text and left-align them in the cell.

Entering Numbers

Valid numbers can include the numeric characters 0–9 and any of these special characters: + – ( ) , $ % . . Numbers are automatically right-aligned. You can include commas, decimal points, dollar signs, percentage signs, and parentheses in the values that you enter.

Although you can include punctuation, you may not want to. For example, rather than type a column of dollar amounts including the dollar signs and decimal points, you can type numbers such as 700 and 81.2, and then format the column with currency formatting. Excel would then change your entries to $700.00 and $81.20, respectively. Refer to Lesson 13 for more information.

To enter a number:

1. Select the cell into which you want to enter a number.

2. Type the number. To enter a negative number, precede it with a minus sign, or surround it with parentheses.

3. Click on the Enter button on the formula bar, or press Enter.

####### If you enter a number, and it appears in the cell as all number signs, don't worry—the number is okay. The cell is not wide enough to display the number. For a quick fix, select the cell, and choose Format Column AutoFit Selection. For more information, refer to Lesson 16.

Entering Dates and Times

You can enter dates and times in a variety of formats. When you enter a date using a format shown in Table 6.1, Excel converts the date into a number which represents the number of days since January 1, 1900. Although you won't see this number (Excel displays it as a normal date), the number is used whenever a calculation involves a date.

Table 6.1 Valid formats for dates and times.

Format	Example
MM/DD/YY	4/8/58 or 04/08/58
MMM-YY	Jan-92
DD-MMM-YY	28-Oct-91
DD-MMM	6-Sep
HH:MM	16:50
HH:MM:SS	8:22:59
HH:MM AM/PM	7:45 PM
HH:MM:SS AM/PM	11:45:16 AM
MM/DD/YY HH:MM	11/8/80 4:20
HH:MM MM/DD/YY	4:20 11/18/80

To enter a date or time:

1. Select the cell into which you want to enter a date or time.

2. Type the date or time in the format in which you want it displayed.

3. Click on the Enter button on the formula bar, or press Enter.

To Dash or to Slash   You can use dashes (–) or slashes (/) when typing dates. Capitalization is not important. For example, 21 FEB becomes 21–Feb. By the way, FEB 21 also becomes 21–Feb.

Day or Night?   Unless you type AM or PM, Excel assumes that you are using a 24-hour military clock. Therefore, 8:20 is assumed to be AM, not PM. If you type 8:20 PM, Excel inserts the military time equivalent: 20:20.

Entering Data Quickly

Excel offers several features for helping you copy entries into several cells.

- To copy an existing entry into several surrounding cells, you can use the Fill feature.

- To have Excel insert a sequence of entries in neighboring cells (for example Monday, Tuesday, Wednesday), you can use AutoFill.

- To have Excel calculate and insert a series of entries according to your specifications (for example 5, 10, 15, 20), you can fill with a series.

These features are explained in greater detail in the following sections.

Copying Entries with Fill

You can copy an existing entry into any surrounding cells, by performing the following steps:

1. Select the cell whose contents and formatting you want to copy.

2. Position the mouse pointer over the selected cell, and drag it over all the cells into which you want to copy the cell entry.

3. Open the Edit menu, and select Fill. The Fill submenu appears.

4. Select the direction in which you want to copy the entry. For example, if you choose Right, Excel inserts the entry into the selected cells to the right.

An easier way to fill is to drag the fill handle in the lower right corner of the selected cell to highlight the cells into which you want to copy the entry (see Figure 6.2). When you release the mouse button, the contents and formatting of the original cell are copied to the selected cells.

Copying Across Worksheets   You can copy the contents and/or formatting of cells from one worksheet to one or more worksheets in the workbook. To copy to worksheets, first select the worksheet you want to copy from and the worksheets you want to copy to (see Lesson 5). Then, select the cells you want to copy. Open the Edit menu, select Fill, and select Across Worksheets. Select All (to copy the cells' contents and formatting), Contents, or Formats, and select OK.

Smart Copying with AutoFill

Unlike Fill, which merely copies an entry to one or more cells, AutoFill copies intelligently. For example, if you want to enter the days of the week (Sunday through Saturday), you type the first entry (Sunday), and AutoFill inserts the other entries for you. Try it:

1. Type Monday into a cell.

2. Drag the fill handle up, down, left, or right to select six more cells.

3. Release the mouse button. Excel inserts the remaining days of the week, in order, into the selected cells (see Figure 6.3).

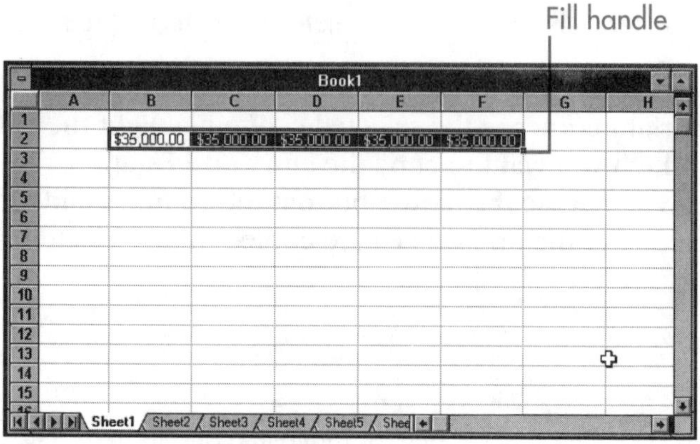

Fill handle

Figure 6.2 Drag the fill handle to copy the contents and formatting into neighboring cells.

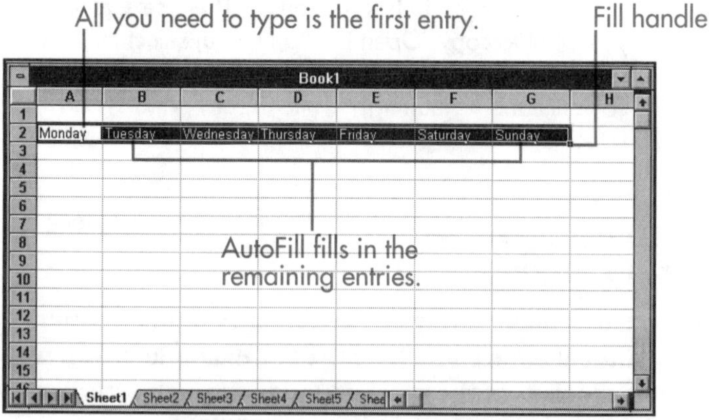

All you need to type is the first entry.   Fill handle

AutoFill fills in the remaining entries.

Figure 6.3 Drag the fill handle over the cells you want to fill.

Excel has the days of the week stored as an
AutoFill entry. You can store your own series as
AutoFill entries. Here's how you do it:

1. Open the Tools menu, and choose Options.
   The Options dialog box appears.

2. Click on the Custom Lists tab. The selected
   tab moves up front, as shown in Figure 6.4.

3. Click on the Add button. An insertion point
   appears in the List Entries text box.

4. Type the entries you want to use for your
   AutoFill entries (for example, Q1, Q2, Q3,
   Q4). Press Enter at the end of each entry.

5. Click on the OK button.

Type your entries here.
Press Enter after each entry.

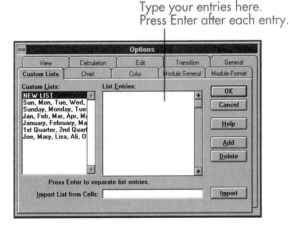

Figure 6.4 Excel lets you create your own AutoFill series.

Now that you have your own AutoFill entry, you can
type any item in the list and use AutoFill to insert the remaining entries.

**Transforming Existing Entries to
AutoFill** If you have already typed the entries
you want to use for your AutoFill entries, select
the entries before you choose Options from the
Tools menu. Click on the Custom Lists tab, and select the
Import button. Excel lifts the selected entries from your
worksheet and sticks them in the List Entries text box.

More Control with Series

Although AutoFill is good for a brief series of entries, you
may encounter situations in which you need more control or
need to fill lots of cells with incremental entries. In such
situations, you should use the series feature. Excel recog-
nizes four types of series, shown in Table 6.2.

Table 6.2 Data series.

Series	Initial Entry	Resulting Series
Linear	1,2	3,4,5
	100,99	98,97,96
	1,3	5,7,9
Growth	10 (step 5)	15,20,25
	10 (step 10)	20,30,40
Date	Mon	Tue, Wed, Thur
	Feb	Mar, Apr, May
	Qtr1	Qtr2, Qtr3, Qtr4
	1992	1993, 1994, 1995
Autofill	Team 1	Team 2, Team 3, Team 4
	Qtr 4	Qtr 1, Qtr 2, Qtr 3
	1st Quarter	2nd Quarter, 3rd Quarter, 4th Quarter

Here's what you do to create a series:

1. Enter a value in one cell. This value will be the starting or ending value in the series.

2. Select the cells into which you want to extend the series.

3. Pull down the Edit menu, select Fill, and select Series. The Series dialog box, shown in Figure 6.5, appears.

4. Under Series in, select Rows or Columns. This tells Excel whether to fill down a column or across a row.

5. Under Type, choose a series type. (Look back at Table 6.2.)

6. Adjust the Step value (amount between each series value), and Stop value (last value you want Excel to enter), if necessary.

7. Click on OK, or press Enter, and the series is created.

Figure 6.5   The Series dialog box.

Editing Data

After you have entered data into a cell, you may change it by editing. To replace an entry, simply select the cell and start typing.

In-Cell Editing In previous versions of Excel, you had to edit an entry in the formula bar. In Excel 5.0, you can display the insertion point in either the formula bar or in the cell itself.

To edit an entry, do this:

1. Select the cell in which you want to edit data.

2. Position the insertion point in the formula bar with the mouse, or press F2, or double-click on the cell. This puts you in Edit mode; Edit appears in the status bar.

3. Press ← or → to move the insertion point. Use the Backspace key to delete characters to the left, or the Delete key to delete characters to the right. Type any additional characters.

4. Click on the Enter button on the formula bar, or press Enter to accept your changes.

Spell Checking Excel 5.0 offers a spell checking feature. To run the spell checker, open the Tools menu, and select Spelling, or click on the Spelling button in the Standard toolbar. For more information, click on the Help button when the Spelling dialog box appears.

Undoing an Action

You can undo almost anything you do in a worksheet, including any change you enter into a cell. To undo a change, do one of the following:

• Open the Edit menu, and choose Undo.

• Press Ctrl+Z.

- Click on the Undo button in the Standard toolbar. (This is the button with the counterclockwise arrow on it.)

  To undo an Undo (reverse a change), take one of these actions:

- Open the Edit menu, and select Redo.

- Click on the Repeat button in the Standard toolbar. (This is the button with the clockwise arrow on it.)

Undo/Repeat One Act   The Undo and Repeat features only undo or repeat the most recent action you took.

In this lesson, you learned how to enter different types of data, how to automate data entry, and how to make changes and undo those changes.

Lesson

Working with Ranges

In this lesson, you will learn how to select and name cell ranges.

What Is a Range?

A range is a rectangular group of connected cells. The cells in a range may all be in a column, or a row, or any combination of columns and rows, as long as the range forms a rectangle, as shown in Figure 7.1.

Learning how to use ranges can save you time. For example, you can select a range and use it to format a group of cells with one step. You can use a range to print only a selected group of cells. You can also use ranges in formulas.

Ranges are referred to by their anchor points (the top left corner and the lower right corner). For example, the ranges shown in Figure 7.1 are B4:D7, A9:D9, and E2.

Selecting a Range

To select a range, use the mouse:

1. Move the mouse pointer to the upper left corner of a range.

2. Click and hold the left mouse button.

3. Drag the mouse to the lower right corner of the range and release the mouse button.

4. To select the same range of cells on more than one worksheet, select the worksheets (see Lesson 5).

5. Release the mouse button. The selected range will be highlighted.

> **A Quick Selection** To quickly select a row or a column, click on the row number or column letter at the edge of the worksheet. To select the entire worksheet, click on the rectangle above row 1 and left of column A.

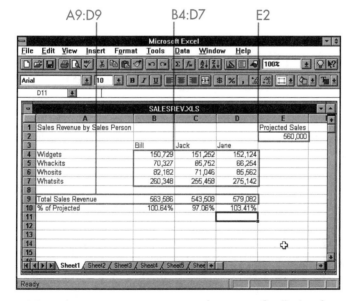

Figure 7.1 A range is any combination of cells that forms a rectangle.

Naming a Cell Range

Up to this point, you have used cell addresses to refer to cells. Although that works, it is often more convenient to name cells with more recognizable names. For example, say you want to determine your net income by subtracting expenses from income. You can name the cell that contains your total income INCOME, and name the cell that contains your total expenses EXPENSES. You can then determine your net income by using the formula:

=INCOME–EXPENSES

to make the formula more logical and easier to manage. Naming cells and ranges also makes it easier to cut, copy, and move blocks of cells, as explained in Lessons 8 and 9.

To name a cell range:

1. Select the range of cells you want to name. Make sure all the cells are on the same worksheet.

2. Click inside the name box (left side of the formula bar). See Figure 7.2.

3. Type a range name (up to 255 characters). Valid names can include letters, numbers, periods, and underlines, but NO spaces.

4. Press Enter.

Another way to name a range is to select it and then open the Insert menu, and select Name Define. This displays the Define Name dialog box, shown in Figure 7.3. Type a name in the Names in Workbook text box, and click on OK. This dialog box also lets you delete names.

Name box   Selected range

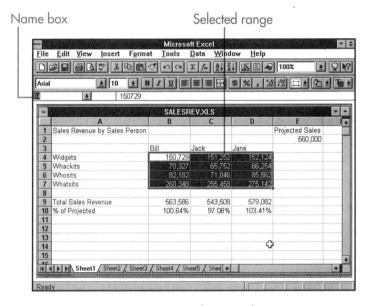

Figure 7.2 Type a name in the name box.

Type a
name here.

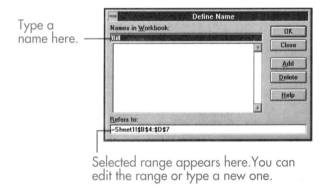

Selected range appears here. You can
edit the range or type a new one.

Figure 7.3 The Define Name dialog box.

In this lesson, you learned how to select and name
ranges. In the next lesson, you will learn how to copy, move,
and erase data.

Lesson

8

Copying, Moving, and Erasing Data

In this lesson, you will learn to organize your worksheet to meet your changing needs by copying, moving, and erasing data.

When you copy or move data, a copy of that data is placed in a temporary storage area called the Clipboard.

> **What Is the Clipboard?**   The Clipboard is an area of memory that is accessible to all Windows programs. The Clipboard is used by all Windows programs to copy or move data from place to place within a program, or between programs. The techniques that you learn here are the same ones used in all Windows programs.

Copying Data

You make copies of data to use in other sections of your worksheet or in other worksheets or workbooks. The original data remains in place, and a copy of it is placed where you indicate.

To copy data:

1. Select the range or cell that you want to copy.

2. Pull down the Edit menu, and select Copy, or press Ctrl+C. The contents of the selected cell(s) are copied to the Clipboard.

3. Select the first cell in the area where you would like to place the copy. (To copy the data to another worksheet or workbook, change to that worksheet or workbook.)

4. Pull down the Edit menu, and choose Paste, or press Ctrl+V.

Watch Out! When copying or moving data, be careful when you indicate the range where the data should be pasted. Excel will paste the data over any existing data in the indicated range.

You can copy the same data to several places in the worksheet by repeating the Edit Paste command. Data copied to the Clipboard remains there until you copy or cut something else.

Cut, Copy, and Paste Buttons When copying and pasting data, don't forget the Standard toolbar. It includes buttons for cutting, copying, and pasting data, allowing you to bypass the menu system.

Quick Copying with Drag & Drop The fastest way to copy is to use the Drag & Drop feature. Select the cells you want to copy, and then hold down the Ctrl key while dragging the cell selector border where you want the cells copied (see

Figure 8.1). When you release the mouse button, the contents are copied to the new location. If you forget to hold down the Ctrl key, Excel moves the data rather than copying it.

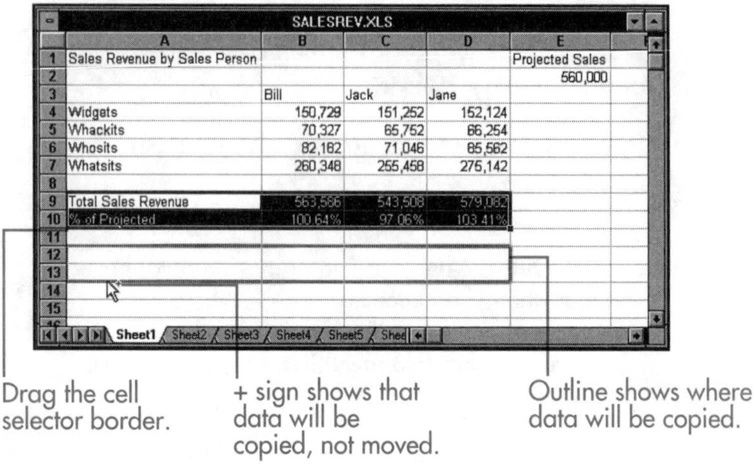

Drag the cell selector border.   + sign shows that data will be copied, not moved.   Outline shows where data will be copied.

Figure 8.1 Hold down the Ctrl key while dragging the cell selector border.

Moving Data

Moving data is similar to copying, except that the data is removed from its original place and moved to the new location.

To move data:

1. Select the range or cell that you want to move.

2. Pull down the Edit menu, and select Cut, or press Ctrl+X.

3. Select the first cell in the area where you would like to place the data. To move the data to another worksheet, change to that worksheet.

4. Pull down the Edit menu, and select Paste, or press Ctrl+V.

Move It Fast! To move data quickly, use the Drag & Drop feature. Select the data to be moved, and then drag the cell selector border without holding down the Ctrl key.

Shortcut Menu When cutting, copying, and pasting data, don't forget the shortcut menu. Simply select the cells you want to cut or copy, and then right-click on the selected cells.

Erasing Data

Although erasing data is fairly easy, you must decide exactly what you want to erase first. Here are your choices:

- Use the **Edit Clear** command to erase only the contents or formatting of the cells. The **Edit Clear** command is covered next.

- Use the **Edit Delete** command to remove the cells and everything in them. This is covered in Lesson 9.

With the **Clear** command, you can remove the data from a cell, or just its formula, formatting, or attached notes. Here's what you do:

1. Select the range of cells you wish to clear.

2. Pull down the Edit menu, and choose Clear. The Clear submenu appears, as shown in Figure 8.2.

3. Select the desired clear option: **All** (clears formats, contents, and notes), **Formats**, **Contents**, or **Notes**.

A Clean Slate To quickly clear the contents of cells, select the cells and press the Delete key.

Clear submenu

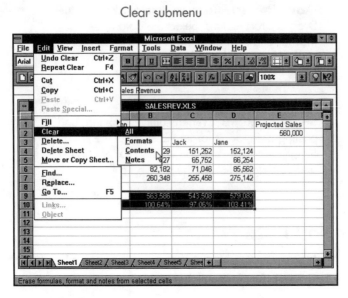

Figure 8.2 The Clear submenu.

Shortcut Menu When clearing cells, don't forget the shortcut menu. Select the cells you want to clear, right-click on one of them, and then choose Delete.

In this lesson, you learned how to copy and move data. You also learned how to clear data from cells. In the next lesson, you will learn how to insert and delete cells, rows, and columns.

Inserting and Deleting Cells, Rows, and Columns

In this lesson, you will learn how to rearrange your worksheet by adding and deleting cells, rows, and columns.

Inserting Cells

Sometimes, you will need to insert information into a worksheet, right in the middle of existing data. With the Insert command, you can insert one or more cells, or entire rows and columns.

> **Shifting Cells** Inserting cells in the middle of existing data will cause those other cells to shift down a row or over a column. If you added formulas to your worksheet that rely on the contents of the shifting cells, this could throw off the calculations.

To insert a single cell or a group of cells:

1. Select the cell(s) where you want the new cell(s) inserted. Excel will insert the same number of cells as you select.

2. Pull down the Insert menu, and choose Cells. The Insert dialog box shown in Figure 9.1 appears.

3. Select Shift Cells Right or Shift Cells Down.

4. Click on OK, or press Enter. Excel inserts the cell(s) and shifts the data in the other cells in the specified direction.

Figure 9.1   The Insert dialog box.

> **Drag Insert**   A quick way to insert cells is to hold down the Shift key while dragging the fill handle (the little box in the lower right corner of the selected cell(s)). Drag the fill handle up, down, left, or right to set the position of the new cells.

Inserting Rows and Columns

Inserting entire rows and columns in your worksheet is similar to inserting a cell(s). Here's what you do:

1. Do one of the following:

    • To insert a single row or column, select a cell. Columns are inserted to the left of the current cell. Rows are inserted above the current cell.

    • Select the number of columns or rows you want to insert. To select columns, drag over the column letters at the top of the worksheet. To select rows, drag over the row numbers.

2. Open the Insert menu.

3. Select Rows or Columns. Excel inserts the row(s) or column(s) and shifts the adjacent rows down or adjacent columns right. Figure 9.2 simulates a worksheet before and after a row is inserted.

> **Shortcut Insert** To quickly insert rows or columns, select one or more rows or columns, and then right-click on one of them. Choose Insert from the shortcut menu.

Before inserting a row

	A	B	C	D	E	
			SALESREV.XLS			
1	Sales Revenue by Sales Person				Projected Sales	
2					560,000	
3		Bill	Jack	Jane		
4	Widgets	150,729	151,252	152,124		
5	Whackits	70,327	65,752	66,254		
6	Whosits	82,182	71,046	85,562		
7	Whatsits	260,348	255,458	275,142		
8						
9		Bill	Jack	Jane		
10	Widgets	150,729	151,252	152,124		
11						
12	Whackits	70,327	65,752	66,254		
13	Whosits	82,182	71,046	85,562		
14	Whatsits	260,348	255,458	275,142		
15						

Sheet1 / Sheet2 / Sheet3 / Sheet4 / Sheet5 / Shee

After inserting a row

Figure 9.2   Inserting a row in a worksheet.

Deleting Cells

In Lesson 8, you learned how to clear the contents and formatting of selected cells. This merely removed what was inside the cells. If you want to remove the cells completely, perform the following steps:

1. Select the range of cells you want to delete.

2. Pull down the Edit menu, and choose Delete. The Delete dialog box appears, as shown in Figure 9.3.

3. Select the desired Delete option: Shift Cells **L**eft, Shift Cells **U**p, Entire **R**ow, or Entire **C**olumn.

Figure 9.3 The Delete dialog box asks where you want surrounding cells shifted.

Deleting Rows and Columns

Deleting rows and columns is similar to deleting cells. When you delete a row, the rows below the deleted row move up to fill the space. When you delete a column, the columns to the right shift left.

To delete a row or column:

1. Click on the row number or column letter of the row or column you want to delete. You can select more than one row or column by dragging over the row numbers or column letters.

2. Pull down the Edit menu, and choose Delete. Excel deletes the row(s) or column(s). Figure 9.4 simulates a worksheet before and after a row was deleted.

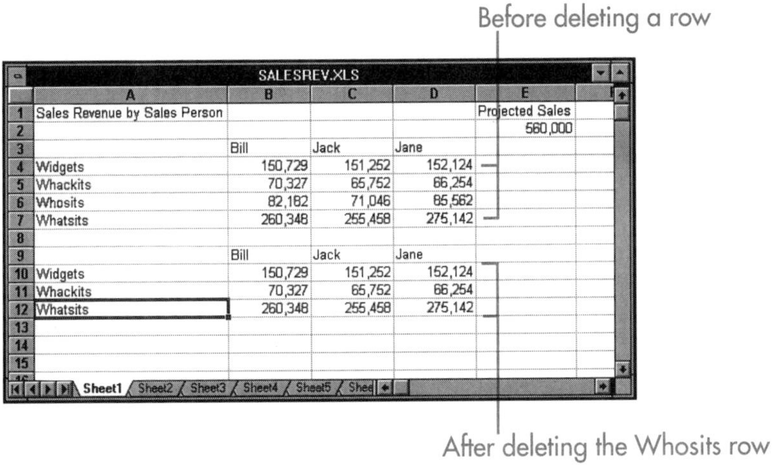

Before deleting a row

After deleting the Whosits row

Figure 9.4   Deleting a row in a worksheet.

In this lesson, you learned how to insert and delete rows and columns. In the next lesson, you will learn how to use formulas.

Lesson

Writing Formulas

In this lesson, you will learn how to use formulas to calculate results in your worksheets.

What Is a Formula?

Worksheets use formulas to perform calculations on the data you enter. With formulas, you can perform addition, subtraction, multiplication, and division using the values contained in various cells.

Formulas typically consist of one or more cell addresses and/or values and a mathematical operator, such as + (addition), – (subtraction), * (multiplication), or / (division). For example, if you wanted to determine the average of the three values contained in cells A1, B1, and C1, you would use the following formula:

=(A1+B1+C1)/3

Start Right   Every formula must begin with an equal sign (=).

Figure 10.1 shows several formulas in action. Table 10.1 lists the mathematical operators you can use to create formulas.

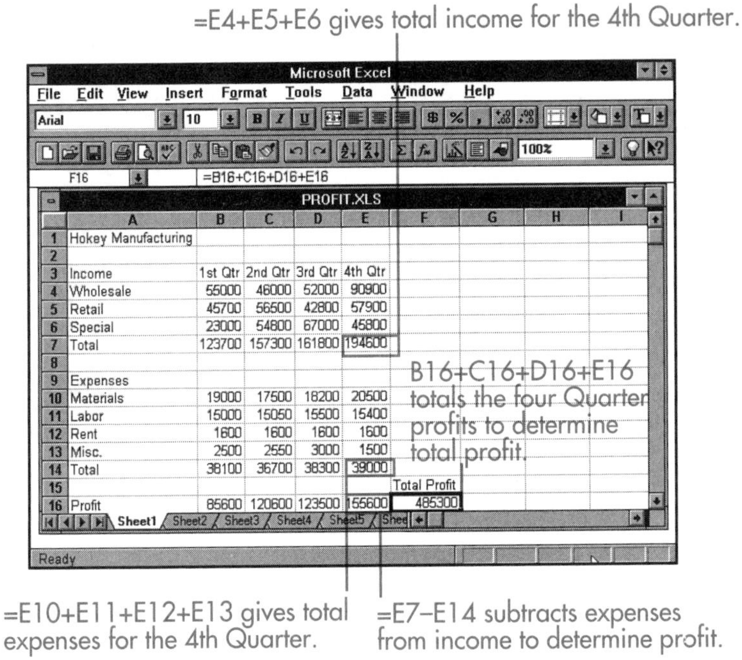
=E4+E5+E6 gives total income for the 4th Quarter.
Microsoft Excel
=B16+C16+D16+E16
PROFIT.XLS
B16+C16+D16+E16 totals the four Quarter profits to determine total profit.
Total Profit
=E10+E11+E12+E13 gives total expenses for the 4th Quarter.
=E7–E14 subtracts expenses from income to determine profit.

Figure 10.1 Type a formula in the cell where you want the resulting value to appear.

Table 10.1 Excel's mathematical operators.

Operator	Performs	Sample	Result Formula
^	Exponentiation	=A1^3	Enters the result of raising the value in cell A1 to the third power.
+	Addition	=A1+A2	Enters the total of the values in cells A1 and A2.

continues

Table 10.1 Continued

Operator	Performs	Sample	Result Formula
–	Subtraction	=A1–A2	Subtracts the value in cell A2 from the value in cell A1.
*	Multiplication	=A2*3	Multiplies the value in cell A2 by 3.
/	Division	=A1/50	Divides the value in cell A1 by 50.
	Combination	=(A1+A2+A3)/3	Determines the average of the values in cells A1 through A3.

Order of Operations

Excel performs a series of operations from left to right in the following order, giving some operators *precedence* over others:

1st	Exponential equations
2nd	Multiplication and division
3rd	Addition and subtraction

This is important to keep in mind when you are creating equations, because the order of operations determines the result.

For example, if you want to determine the average of the values in cells A1, B1, and C1, and you enter =A1+B1+C1/3, you'll probably get the wrong answer. The value in C1 will be divided by 3, and that result will be added to A1+B1. To determine the total of A1 through C1 first, you must enclose that group of values in parentheses: =(A1+B1+C1)/3.

Entering Formulas

You can enter formulas in either of two ways: by *typing* the formula or by *selecting* cell references. To type a formula, perform the following steps:

1. Select the cell in which you want the formula's calculation to appear.

2. Type the equal sign (=).

3. Type the formula. The formula appears in the formula bar.

4. Press Enter, and the result is calculated.

To enter a formula by selecting cell references, take the following steps:

1. Select the cell in which you want the formula's result to appear.

2. Type the equal sign (=).

3. Click on the cell whose address you want to appear first in the formula. The cell address appears in the formula bar.

4. Type a mathematical operator after the value to indicate the next operation you want to perform. The operator appears in the formula bar.

5. Continue clicking on cells and typing operators until the formula is complete.

6. Press Enter to accept the formula or Esc to cancel the operation.

> **Error!**   Make sure that you did not commit one of these common errors: trying to divide by zero or a blank cell, referring to a blank cell, deleting a cell being used in a formula, or using a range name when a single cell address is expected.

Displaying Formulas

Excel does not display the actual formula in a cell. Instead, Excel displays the result of the calculation. You can view the formula, by selecting the cell and looking in the formula bar. If you want to see the formulas in the cells, do this:

1. Open the Tools menu, and choose Options.

2. Click on the View tab.

3. Click on the Formulas check box. An **X** appears, indicating that the option has been turned on.

4. Click on OK, or press Enter.

> **Display Formulas Quickly**   Use the keyboard shortcut, Ctrl+`, to toggle between viewing formulas or values. Hold down the Ctrl key, and press ` (the accent key—it's the key with the tilde (~) on it).

Editing Formulas

Editing formulas is the same as editing any entry in Excel. Here's how you do it:

1. Select the cell that contains the formula you want to edit.

2. Position the insertion point in the formula bar with the mouse, or press F2 to enter Edit mode.

Quick In-Cell Editing   To quickly edit the contents of a cell, simply double-click on the cell. The insertion point appears inside the cell.

3. Press ← or → to move the insertion point. Use the Backspace key to delete characters to the left, or the Delete key to delete characters to the right. Type any additional characters.

4. Click on the Enter button on the formula bar, or press Enter to accept your changes.

Copying Formulas

Copying formulas is similar to copying other data in a worksheet. (For more details, refer to Lesson 8.) To copy formulas:

1. Select the cell that contains the formula you want to copy.

2. Pull down the Edit menu, and select Copy, or press Ctrl+C.

3. Select the cell(s) into which you want to copy the formula. To copy the formula to another worksheet or workbook, change to it.

4. Pull down the Edit menu, and select Paste, or press Ctrl+V.

> **Drag and Drop Formulas**   To quickly copy a formula, use the Drag & Drop feature. Select the cell that contains the formula you want to copy, and then hold down the Ctrl key while dragging the cell selector border where you want the formula copied. When you release the mouse button, the formula is copied to the new location. If you need to copy one formula into two or more cells, use the AutoFill feature as explained in Lesson 6.

> **Get an Error?**   If you get an error after copying a formula, verify the cell references in the copied formula. See the next section, "Using Relative and Absolute Cell Addresses," for more details.

Using Relative and Absolute Cell Addresses

When you copy a formula from one place in the worksheet to another, Excel adjusts the cell references in the formulas relative to their new positions in the worksheet. For example, in Figure 10.2, cell B9 contains the formula **=B4+B5+B6+B7**, which determines the total sales revenue for Bill. If you copy that formula to cell C9 (to determine the total sales revenue for Jack), Excel would automatically change the formula to **=C4+C5+C6+C7**.

Cell references are adjusted for column C.

	A	B	C	D	E
1	Sales Revenue by Sales Person				Projected Sales
2					560,000
3		Bill	Jack	Jane	
4	Widgets	150,729	151,252	152,124	
5	Whackits	70,327	85,752	86,254	
6	Whosits	82,182	71,046	85,562	
7	Whatsits	260,348	255,458	275,142	
8					
9	Total Sales Revenue	563,586	543,508	579,082	
10	% of Projected	100.64%	97.06%	103.41%	
11					
12					
13					
14					
15					

C9   =C4+C5+C6+C7

Figure 10.2   Excel adjusts cell references when copying formulas.

Sometimes, you may not want the cell references to be adjusted when formulas are copied. That's when absolute references become important.

> **Absolute vs. Relative**   An *absolute refer-ence* is a cell reference in a formula that does not change when copied to a new location. A *relative reference* is a cell reference in a formula that is adjusted when the formula is copied.

The formula in cells B10, C10, and D10 uses an absolute reference to cell E2, which holds the projected sales for this year. (B10, C10, and D10 divide the sums from row 9 of each column by the contents of cell E2.) If you didn't use an absolute reference, when you copied the formula from B10 to C10, the cell reference would be incorrect, and you would get an error message.

To make a cell reference in a formula absolute, you must add a $ (dollar sign) before the letter and number that make up the cell address. For example, the formula in B10 would read as follows:

B9/E2

You can type the dollar signs yourself or press F4 after typing the cell address. Some formulas use mixed references. For example, the column letter may be an absolute reference and the row number may be a relative reference, as in the formula $A2/2. If you had this formula in cell C2, and you copied it to cell D10, the result would be the formula $A10/2. The row reference (row number) would be adjusted, but not the column.

> **Mixed References**   A reference that is only partially absolute, such as A$2 or $A2, is called a *mixed reference*. When a formula that uses a mixed reference is copied to another cell, only part of the cell reference is adjusted.

Changing the Recalculation Setting

Excel recalculates the formulas in a worksheet every time you edit a value in a cell. However, on a large worksheet, you may not want Excel to recalculate until you have entered all your changes. To change the recalculation setting, take the following steps:

1. Open the Tools menu, and choose Options.

2. Click on the Calculation tab.

3. Select one of the following Calculation options:

Automatic is the default setting. It recalculates the entire workbook each time you edit or enter a formula.

Automatic Except **Tables** automatically recalculates everything except formulas in a data table. You'll learn about data tables in Lesson 21.

Manual tells Excel to recalculate only when you say so. To recalculate, you must press F9 or choose Tools Options Calculation Calc Now. If you choose **Manual**, you can turn the Recalculate before Save option off or on.

4. Click on the OK button.

   In this lesson, you learned how to enter and edit formulas. You also learned when to use relative and absolute cell addresses. In the next lesson, you will learn how to use Excel's Function Wizard to insert more complex formulas.

Lesson

Performing Complex Calculations with Functions

In this lesson, you will learn how to perform complex calculations with functions and how to use Excel's new Function Wizard to quickly insert functions in cells.

What Are Functions?

Functions are complex ready-made formulas that perform a series of operations on a specified *range* of values. For example, to determine the sum of a series of numbers in cells A1 through H1, you can enter the function =SUM(A1:H1), instead of entering =A1+B1+C1+ and so on. Functions can use range references (such as B1:B3), range names (such as SALES), and/or numerical values (such as 585.86).

Every function consists of the following three elements:

- The = sign indicates that what follows is a function.

- The **function name** (for example, SUM) indicates the operation that will be performed.

- The **argument**, for example (A1:H1), indicates the cell addresses of the values that the function will act on. The argument is often a range of cells, but it can be much more complex.

You can enter functions either by typing them in cells or by using the Function Wizard, as you'll see later in this lesson.

Using the AutoSum Tool

Because SUM is one of the most commonly used functions, Excel created a fast way to enter it—you simply click on the AutoSum button in the Standard toolbar. AutoSum guesses what cells you want summed, based on the currently selected cell. If AutoSum selects an incorrect range of cells, you can edit the selection.

To use AutoSum:

1. Select the cell in which you want the sum inserted. Try to choose a cell at the end of a row or column of data.

2. Click on the AutoSum tool in the Standard toolbar. AutoSum inserts =SUM and the range of the cells to the left of or above the selected cell (see Figure 11.1).

3. You can adjust the range of cells by doing one of the following:

   • Click inside the selected cell or the formula bar, and edit the range.

   • Drag the mouse pointer over the correct range of cells.

4. Click on the Enter box in the formula bar, or press Enter. The total for the selected range is calculated.

AutoSum selects a range of cells above
or to the left of the selected cell.   AutoSum button

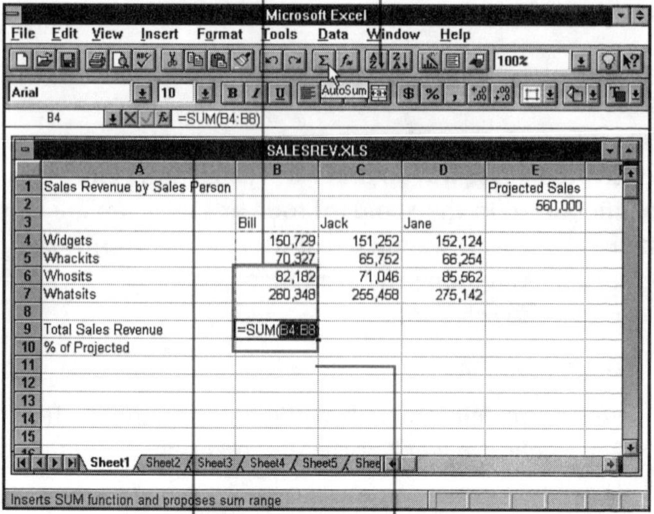

SUM function appears in the   The selected range is inserted
selected cell and in the formula bar. as the function's argument.

Figure 11.1 AutoSum inserts the SUM function and selects
the cells it plans to total.

Using Function Wizard

Although you can type a function directly into a
cell, just as you can type formulas, you may
find it easier to use the Function Wizard. The
Function Wizard is a new feature that leads
you through the process of inserting a function. Here's
how you do it:

1. Select the cell in which you want to insert the function. (You can insert a function by itself or as part of a formula.)

2. Open the Insert menu, and choose Function, or click on the Function Wizard button (the fx button) on the Standard toolbar or formula bar. The Function Wizard – Step 1 of 2 dialog box appears, as shown in Figure 11.2.

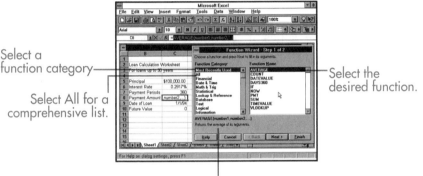

Select a function category

Select All for a comprehensive list.

Select the desired function.

Look here for a description of the highlighted function.

Figure 11.2   The first step is to select the function you want to use.

Function Names   If this is your first encounter with functions, don't expect them to be simple. However, you can learn a lot about a function and what it does by reading the descriptions in the dialog box. Whenever you highlight a function name, Excel displays a description of the function. If you need more help, click on the Help button, or press F1.

3. In the Function Category list, select the type of function you want to insert. Excel displays the names of the available functions in the Function Name list.

4. Select the function you want to insert from the Function Name list, and then click on the Next button. Excel displays the Step 2 of 2 dialog box. This box will differ depending on the selected function. Figure 11.3 shows the dialog box you'll see if you chose the PMT function.

5. Enter the values or cell ranges for the argument. You can type a value or argument, or drag the dialog box title bar out of the way and click on the desired cells with the mouse pointer.

The function and argument appear on the formula bar and the selected cell.   The result appears here.

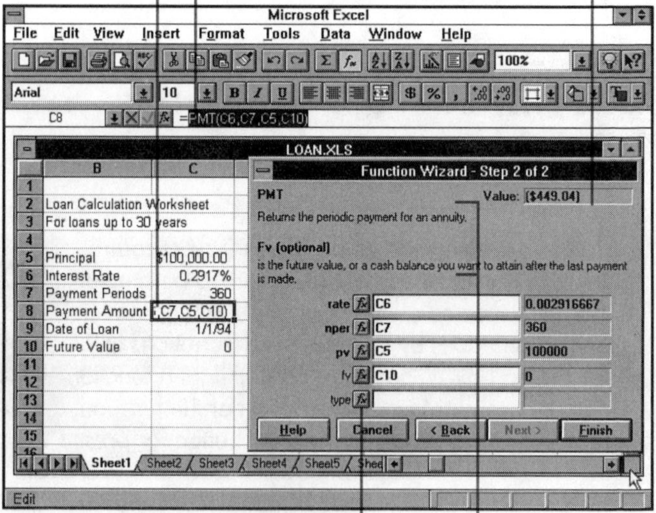

These fx buttons let you put functions inside functions (up to seven deep).   Look here for help, or click on the Help button.

Figure 11.3 The second step is to enter the values and cell references that make up the argument.

6. Click on the Finish button. Excel inserts the function and argument in the selected cell and displays the result.

> **Low Interest Rates**   If the interest rate shown in Figure 11.3 looks too good to be true, it's because Excel works with monthly percentage rates rather than annual percentage rates. Whenever you enter a percent on a loan or investment, enter the annual percentage rate divided by 12. For example, if your mortgage is at 7% (.07), you would enter =.07/12.

To edit a function, you can type your corrections just as you can with a formula. You can also use the Function Wizard. To use the Wizard, select the cell that contains the function you want to edit. (You want the cell selected, but you don't want to be in Edit mode; that is, the insertion point should not be displayed in the cell.) Open the Insert menu, and choose Function, or click on the Function Wizard button. The Editing Function 1 of 1 dialog box appears, allowing you to edit the function's argument.

In this lesson, you learned the basics of dealing with functions, and you learned how to use Excel's Function Wizard to quickly enter functions. You also learned how to quickly total a series of numbers with the AutoSum tool. In the next lesson, you will learn how to print your workbook.

Lesson

Printing Your Workbook

In this lesson, you will learn how to print an entire workbook or only a portion of it.

Changing the Page Setup

Before you print a workbook, you should make sure that the page is set up correctly for printing. To do this, open the File menu, and choose Page Setup. You'll see the Page Setup dialog box, as shown in Figure 12.1.

Right-Click on the Workbook Title Bar For quick access to commands that affect a workbook, right-click on the workbook's title bar. For example, to check the page setup, right-click on the title bar, and choose Page Setup.

Figure 12.1 The Page Setup dialog box.

Enter your page setup settings as follows:

Page tab

Orientation   Select Portrait to print from left to right across a page or Landscape to print from top to bottom on a page. (Landscape makes the page wider than it is tall.)

Scaling   You can reduce and enlarge your workbook or force it to fit within a specific page size.

Paper Size   This is 8 1/2 by 11 inches, by default. You can choose a different size from the list.

Print Quality   You can print a draft of your spread-sheet to print quickly and save wear and tear on your printer, or you can print in high quality for a final copy. Print quality is measured in dpi (dots per inch)—the higher the number, the better the print.

First Page Number   You can set the starting page number to something other than 1.

Margins tab

Top, Bottom, Left, Right   You can adjust the size of the left, right, top, and bottom margins.

From Edge   You can specify how far you want a Header or Footer printed from the edge of the page. (You use the Header/Footer tab to add a header or footer to your workbook.)

Center on Page   You can center the printing between the left and right margins (Horizontally) and between the top and bottom margins (Vertically).

Header/Footer tab

Header/Footer   You can add a Header (such as a title, which repeats at the top of each page) or a Footer (such as page numbers, which repeat at the bottom of each page).

Custom Header/Custom Footer   You can choose the Custom Header or Custom Footer button to create headers and footers that insert the time, date, worksheet tab name, and workbook file name.

Print Area   You can print a portion of a workbook or worksheet by entering the range of cells you want to print. You can type the range, or drag the dialog box title bar out of the way and drag the mouse pointer over the desired cells. If you do not select a print area, Excel will print all the cells that contain data.

Print Titles   If you have a row or column of entries that you want repeated as titles on every page, type the range for this row or column, or drag over the cells with the mouse pointer.

Print   You can tell Excel exactly how to print some aspects of the workbook. For example, you can have the gridlines (the lines that define the cells) printed. You can also have a color spreadsheet printed in black-and-white.

Page Order   You can indicate how data in the workbook should be read and printed: in sections from top to bottom or in sections from left to right.

When you are done entering your settings, click on the OK button.

Adjusting Page Breaks

When you print a workbook, Excel determines the page breaks based on the paper size and margins and the selected print area. You may want to override the automatic page breaks with your own breaks. However, before you add page breaks, try these options:

- Adjust the widths of individual columns to make the best use of space (see Lesson 16).

- Consider printing the workbook sideways (using Landscape orientation).

- Change the left, right, top, and bottom margins to smaller values.

If after trying these options, you still want to insert page breaks, first determine whether you need to limit the number of columns on a page or the number of rows.

To limit the number of columns:

1. Select a cell that's in the column to the right of the last column you want on the page. For example, if you want Excel to print only columns A through G on the first page, select a cell in column H.

2. Move to row one of that column.

3. Open the Insert menu, and choose Page Break. A dashed line appears to the left of the selected column, showing the position of the page break.

To limit the number of rows:

1. Select a cell in row just below the last row you want on the page. For example, if you want Excel to print only rows 1 through 12 on the first page, select a cell in row 13.

2. Move to column A of that row.

3. Open the Insert menu, and choose Page Break. A dashed line appears above the selected row.

> **One Step Page Breaks**   You can set the lower right corner of a workbook in one step. Select the cell that is below and to the right of the last cell for the page, and then open the Insert menu, and select Page Break. For example, if you wanted cell G12 to be the last cell on that page, move to cell H13, and set the page break.

> **Remove a Page Break**   To remove a page break, move to the cell that you used to set the page break, open the Insert menu, and choose Remove Page Break.

Previewing a Print Job

After you've determined your page setup, print area, and page breaks (if any), you can preview your print job before you print. To preview a print job, open the File menu, and select Print Preview, or click on the Print Preview button in the Standard toolbar. Your workbook appears as it will when printed, as shown in Figure 12.2.

> **Page Setup Print Preview**   You can also preview a print job when you are setting up a page. When the Page Setup dialog box is displayed, click on the Print Preview button.

To return to the normal workbook window, click on Close.

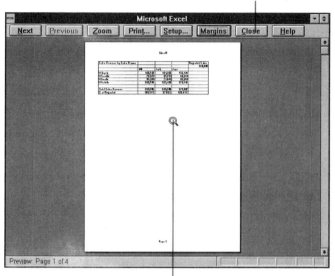

Mouse pointer allows you to zoom
in on a portion of the worksheet.

Figure 12.2   You can preview your workbook before printing it.

A Close-Up View   Zoom in on any area of the preview by clicking on it with the mouse. You can also use the Zoom button.

Printing

After setting the page setup and previewing your data, it is time to print.

To print your workbook:

1. Open the File menu, and select Print (or press Ctrl+P). The Print dialog box appears, as shown in Figure 12.3.

2. Select the options you would like to use:

Print What allows you to print the currently selected cells, the selected worksheets, or the entire workbook.

Copies allows you to print more than one copy of the selection, worksheet, or workbook.

Page Range lets you print one or more pages. For example, if the selected print area will take up 15 pages, and you want to print only pages 5-10, select Page(s), and then type the numbers of the first and last page you want to print in the From and To spin boxes.

3. Click on OK, or press Enter.

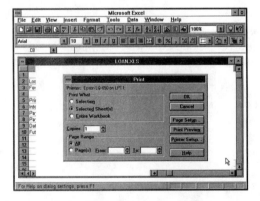

Figure 12.3 The Print dialog box.

Quick Print   To print one copy of all the data in a workbook using the default page setup settings, click on the Print button in the Standard toolbar. Excel bypasses the Print dialog box and immediately starts printing the workbook.

In this lesson, you learned how to print your workbook. In the next lesson, you will learn how to improve the look of your text by adding character and number formatting.

Lesson

Adjusting Number Formats and Text Alignment

In this lesson, you will learn how to customize the appearance of numbers in your worksheet and control the alignment of text inside cells.

Formatting Values

Numeric values are usually more than just numbers. They represent a dollar value, a date, a percent, or some other real value. To indicate what particular values stand for, you must display the value in a certain format. Excel offers a wide range of formats as listed in Table 13.1.

Table 13.1 Excel's numeric formats.

Number Format	Display when you enter:			
	2000	2	–2	.2
General	2000	2	–2	0.2
0	2000	2	–2	0
0.00	2000.00	2.00	–2.00	0.20
#,##0	2,000	2	–2	0
#,##0.00	2,000.00	2.00	–2.00	0.20
$#,##0_);	$2,000	$2	($2)	$0

Number Format	Display when you enter:			
	2000	2	-2	.2
($#,##0)				
$#,##0.00_);	$2,000.00	$2.00	($2.00)	$0.20
($#,##0.00)				
0%	200000%	200%	-200%	20%
0.00%	200000.00%	200.00%	-200.00%	20.00%
0.00E+00	2.00E+03	2.00E+00	-2.00E+00	2.00E-01
#?/ ?	2000	2	-2	1/5

After deciding on a suitable numeric format, follow these steps:

1. Select the cell or range that contains the values you want to format.

2. Pull down the Format menu, and select Cells, or press Ctrl+1. The Format Cells dialog box appears.

3. If the Number tab is not up front, click on it. (See Figure 13.1.)

4. In the Category list, select the numeric format category you want to use. Excel displays the formats in that category in the Format Codes list.

5. In the Format Codes list, select the format code you want to use. When you select a format code, Excel shows you what a sample number would look like formatted with that code.

6. Click on OK, or press Enter.

When you select a category, a list of
format codes for that category appears.

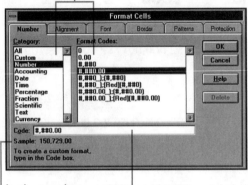

This sample shows what a   You can type your own code
number will look like with   here to create a custom format.
the selected format code.

Figure 13.1   The Format Cells dialog box with the Number
tab up front.

Quick Formatting Techniques   The
Formatting toolbar (just below the Standard
toolbar) contains several buttons for selecting a
number format, including the following: Currency
Style, Percent Style, Comma Style, Increase Decimal, and
Decrease Decimal. You can also change the Number
format of a cell by using the shortcut menu; click the right
mouse button on a cell to display the shortcut menu, and
then choose Format Cells.

Aligning Text in Cells

When you enter data into an Excel worksheet, that data is
aligned automatically. Text is aligned on the left, and
numbers are aligned on the right. Text and numbers are
initially set at the bottom of the cells.

To change the alignment:

1. Select the cell or range you want to align. To center a title or other text over a range of cells, select the entire range of cells in which you want the text centered, including the cell that contains the text.

2. Pull down the Format menu, and select Cells, or press Ctrl+1. The Format Cells dialog box appears.

3. Click on the Alignment tab. The alignment options jump up front as shown in Figure 13.2.

4. Choose from the following options and option groups to set the alignment:

Horizontal lets you specify a left/right alignment in the cell(s). (The Center **across** selection option lets you center a title or other text inside a range of cells.)

Vertical lets you specify how you want the text aligned in relation to the top and bottom of the cell(s).

Orientation lets you flip the text sideways or print it from top to bottom (rather than left to right).

Wrap Text tells Excel to wrap long lines of text within a cell. (Normally, Excel displays all text in a cell on one line.)

5. Click on OK, or press Enter.

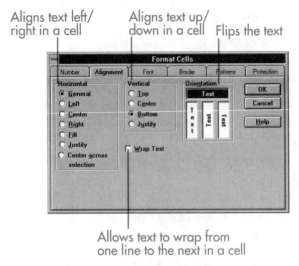

Aligns text left/right in a cell

Aligns text up/down in a cell

Flips the text

Allows text to wrap from one line to the next in a cell

Figure 13.2 The Alignment options.

Alignment Buttons   A quick way to align text and numbers is to use the alignment buttons in the Formatting toolbar. These buttons allow you to align the text Left, Right, Center, or Center Across Columns.

Repeat Performance   To repeat the alignment format command in another cell, use the Repeat Format Cells command from the Edit menu, or click on the Repeat button in the Standard toolbar.

Changing the Default Format and Alignment

When you enter the same type of data into a large worksheet, it is sometimes convenient to change the default format. You then can change the format for only those cells that are exceptions. Note that when you change the default, it affects all the cells in the worksheet.

You can change the default settings for number format, alignment, and others. To change the defaults:

1. Open the Format menu, and choose Style. The Style dialog box appears, as shown in Figure 13.3.

2. In the Style Name list box, select Normal.

3. Click on the Modify button. Excel displays the Format Cells dialog box, as shown in Figure 13.2.

4. Click on the tab for the group of format settings you want to change. For example, you can click on Number to change the default numeric formatting.

5. Select the desired format settings, and then click on the OK button. Excel returns you to the Style dialog box.

6. Click on OK, or press Enter.

Select the Normal style.   The Modify button lets you specify what the style will include.

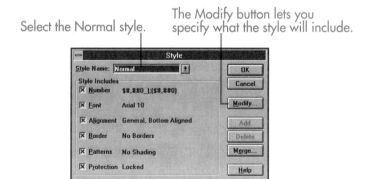

Figure 13.3   The Style dialog box.

In this lesson, you learned how to format numbers and align data in cells. In the next lesson, you will learn how to format text.

Lesson 14

Improving the Look of Your Text

In this lesson, you will learn how to change the appearance of the text in the cells.

How Can You Make Text Look Different?

When you type text or numbers, Excel inserts plain text, which doesn't look very fancy. You can change the following text attributes to improve the appearance of your text or set it apart from other text:

Font For example, System, Roman, and MS Sans Serif.

Font Style For example, Bold, Italic, Underline, and Strikeout.

Size For example, 10-point, 12-point, and 20-point. (There are approximately 72 points in an inch.)

Color For example, Red, Magenta, and Cyan.

What's a Font?   In Excel, a font is a set of characters that have the same typeface, for example, Helvetica. When you select a font, Excel also allows you to change the font's size, add an optional *attribute* to the font, such as bold or italic; underline the text; change its color; or add special effects.

Figure 14.1 shows a worksheet after different attributes have been changed for selected text.

Underline border applied to cells.

Text centered across columns, set in 16-point, bold, italic type, and underlined.

		SALES2.XLS					
	A	B	C	D	E	F	G	H
1			**_Quarterly Sales Report_**					
2								
3			Qtr 1	Qtr 2	Qtr 3	Qtr 4		
4		*John*	$12,052.00	$14,521.00	$17,032.00	$16,054.00		
5		*Charlie*	$9,621.00	$8,751.00	$10,241.00	$10,251.00		
6		*Mary*	$15,083.00	$16,874.00	$14,985.00	$16,745.00		
7		*Jane*	$22,154.00	$22,312.00	$24,569.00	$26,451.00		
8		*Tom*	$21,064.00	$22,064.00	$19,064.00	$25,154.00		
9								
10								
11			Quarterly Sales Report - Projected Sales:			$100,000.00		
12								
13								
14								
15								

Sheet1 / Sheet2 / Sheet3 / Sheet4 / Sheet5 / Shee

Row headings set in italics.

Figure 14.1   A sampling of several text attributes.

Using the Format Cells Dialog Box

You can change the look of your text by using the Format Cells dialog box or by using the Font buttons in the Formatting toolbar. To use the Format Cells dialog box, do this:

1.   Select the cell or range that contains the text you want to format.

2. Open the Format menu, and choose Cells, or press Ctrl+1. (You can also right-click on the selected cells, and choose Format Cells.)

3. Click on the Font tab. The options jump to the front, as shown in Figure 14.2.

4. Enter your font preferences.

5. Click on OK, or press Enter.

Excel uses a default font to style your text as you type it. To change the default font, enter your font preferences in the Font tab, and then click on the Normal Font option. When you click on the OK button, Excel makes your preferences the default font.

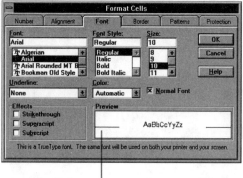

Check the Preview area to see the effects of your choices.

Figure 14.2 The Format Cells dialog box with the Font tab up front.

Font Shortcuts A faster way to change text attributes is to use the keyboard shortcuts. Press Ctrl+B for bold; Ctrl+I for Italic; Ctrl+U for Underline; and Ctrl+5 for Strikethrough.

Changing Text Attributes with Toolbar Buttons

A faster way to enter font changes is to use the buttons and drop-down lists in the Formatting toolbar, as shown in Figure 14.3.

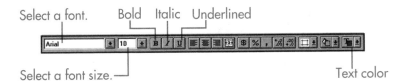

Select a font.   Bold   Italic   Underlined

Select a font size.   Text color

Figure 14.3   Use the Formatting toolbar to quickly enter font changes.

To use a tool to change text attributes:

1. Select the cell or range that contains the text whose look you want to change.

2. To change the font or font size, pull down the appropriate drop-down list, and click on the font or size you want.

3. To add an attribute (such as bold or underlining), click on the desired button.

Change Before You Type   You can activate the attributes you want before you type text. For example, if you want a title in Bold, 12-point MS Sans Serif, set these attributes before you start typing.

In this lesson, you learned how to customize your text to achieve the look you want. In the next lesson, you will learn how to add borders and shading to your worksheet.

Lesson 15

Adding Cell Borders and Shading

In this lesson, you will learn how to add pizzazz to your worksheets by adding borders and shading.

Adding Borders to Cells

As you work with your worksheet on-screen, each cell is identified by a gridline that surrounds the cell. In print, these gridlines may appear washed out. To have better defined lines appear on the printout, you can add borders to selected cells or cell ranges. Figure 15.1 shows the options for adding lines to cells and cell ranges.

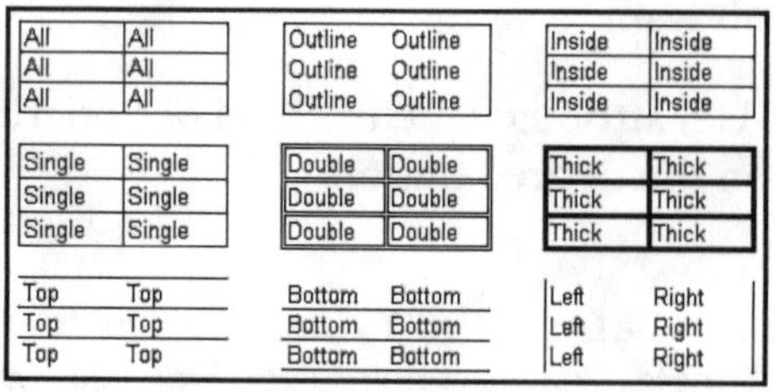

All	All	Outline	Outline	Inside	Inside
All	All	Outline	Outline	Inside	Inside
All	All	Outline	Outline	Inside	Inside

Single	Single	Double	Double	Thick	Thick
Single	Single	Double	Double	Thick	Thick
Single	Single	Double	Double	Thick	Thick

Top	Top	Bottom	Bottom	Left	Right
Top	Top	Bottom	Bottom	Left	Right
Top	Top	Bottom	Bottom	Left	Right

Figure 15.1   A sampling of borders.

To add borders to a cell or range, perform the following steps:

1. Select the cell(s) around which you want a border to appear.

2. Open the Format menu, and choose Cells. The Format Cells dialog box appears.

3. Click on the Border tab. The Border options jump up front, as shown in Figure 15.2.

4. Select the desired border position, style (thickness), and color for the border.

5. Click on OK, or press Enter.

Select a border position.   ┌── Select a border style.

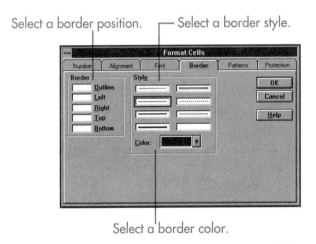

Select a border color.

Figure 15.2 The Format Cells dialog box with the Border tab up front.

Hiding Gridlines   When adding borders to a
worksheet, hide the gridlines to get a better idea
of how the borders will print. Open the Tools
menu, select Options, click on the View tab, and
select Gridlines to remove the **X** from the check box. To
prevent gridlines from printing, open the File menu,
select Page Setup, click on the Sheet tab, and clear the **X**
from the Gridlines check box.

Borders Button   To add borders quickly, select
the cells around which you want the border to
appear, and then click on the arrow to the right
of the Borders button in the Formatting toolbar.
Click on the desired border. If you click on the Borders
button itself (rather than on the arrow), Excel automatically adds a bottom borderline or the borderline you last
selected to the selected cells.

Adding Shading to Cells

For a simple but dramatic effect, add shading to your
worksheets. Figure 15.3 illustrates the effects that you can
create with shading.

To add shading to cell or range:

1.   Select the cell(s) you want to shade.

2.   Pull down the Format menu, and choose Cells.

3.   Click on the Patterns tab. The shading options jump
to the front, as shown in Figure 15.4.

4.   Select the shading color and pattern you want to
use. The **Color** options let you choose a color for
the overall shading. The **Pattern** options let you
select a black-and-white or colored pattern that lies

on top of the overall shading. A preview of the result is displayed in the Sample box.

5. Click on OK, or press Enter.

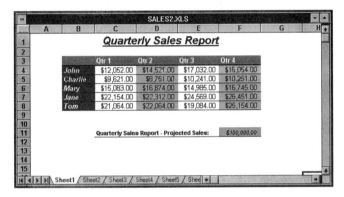

Figure 15.3   A worksheet with added shading.

Select an overall color.

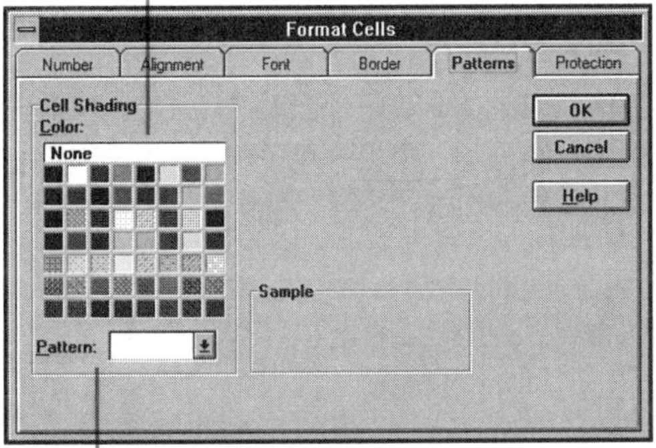

Select a pattern to lay on top of the color.

Figure 15.4   Selecting a shading pattern.

Color Button   A quick way to add shading (without a pattern) is to select the cells you want to shade and then click on the arrow to the right of the Color button (the button that has the bucket on it). Click on the color you want to use. If the shading is dark, consider using the Font Color button (just to the right of the Color button) to select a light color for the text.

More Formatting Tricks

Excel offers a couple of features that take some of the pain out of formatting: AutoFormat and the Format Painter. AutoFormat provides you with several predesigned table formats that you can apply to a worksheet. The Format Painter lets you quickly copy and paste formats that you have already used in a workbook.

To use AutoFormat, perform the following steps:

1. Select the worksheet(s) and cell(s) that contain the data you want to format.

2. Open the Format menu, and choose AutoFormat. The AutoFormat dialog box appears, as shown in Figure 15.5.

3. In the Table Format list, choose the predesigned format you want to use. When you select a format, Excel shows you what it will look like in the Sample area.

4. To exclude certain elements from the AutoFormat, click on the Options button, and choose the formats you want to turn off.

5. Click on the OK button. Excel formats your table to make it look like the one in the preview area.

Select a predesigned table format.

Sample area shows effects of the table format.

AutoFormat		

Table Format:

Simple
Classic 1
Classic 2
Classic 3
Financial 1
Financial 2
Financial 3
Accounting 1
Colorful 1
Colorful 2
Colorful 3

Sample

	Jan	Feb	Mar	Total
East	7	7	5	19
West	6	4	7	17
South	8	7	9	24
Total	21	18	21	60

OK
Cancel
Options >>
Help

Formats to Apply

[X] **N**umber   [X] **F**ont   [X] **A**lignment
[X] **B**order   [X] **P**atterns   [X] **W**idth/Height

Click on the Options button to view the formats that make up the selected table format.

Figure 15.5   Use the AutoFormat dialog box to select a prefab format.

Deformatting an AutoFormat   If you don't like what AutoFormat did to your worksheet, click on the Undo button, or press Ctrl+Z. Or open the Edit menu, and choose Undo AutoFormat.

Excel gives you two ways to copy and paste formatting. You can use the Edit Copy command and then the Edit Paste Special command or the Format Painter button in the Standard toolbar. Because the Format Painter button is faster, I'll give you the steps you need to paint formats:

1.   Select the cell(s) that contain the formatting you want to copy and paste.

2.   Click on the Format Painter button (the one with the paintbrush on it) in the Standard toolbar. Excel copies the formatting. The mouse pointer changes into a paintbrush with a plus sign next to it.

3.   Drag over the cells to which you want to apply the copied formatting.

4.   Release the mouse button. The copied formatting is applied to the selected cells.

In this lesson, you learned some additional ways to enhance the appearance of your worksheets. In the next lesson, you will learn how to change the sizes of rows and columns.

Lesson 16

Changing Column Width and Row Height

In this lesson, you will learn how to adjust the column width and row height to make the best use of the worksheet space. You can set these manually or let Excel make the adjustments for you.

Adjusting Column Width and Row Height with a Mouse

You can adjust the width of a column or the height of a row by using a dialog box or by using the mouse. Here's how you adjust the row height or column width with the mouse:

1. Move the mouse pointer inside the heading for the row or column. To change the row height or column width for two or more rows or columns, drag over the headings with the mouse pointer.

2. Move the mouse pointer to one of the borders, as shown in Figure 16.1. (Use the right border to adjust column width or the bottom border to adjust the row height.)

3. Hold down the mouse button and drag the border.

4. Release the mouse button, and the row height or column width is adjusted.

Dragging the right border of
column C changes its width.

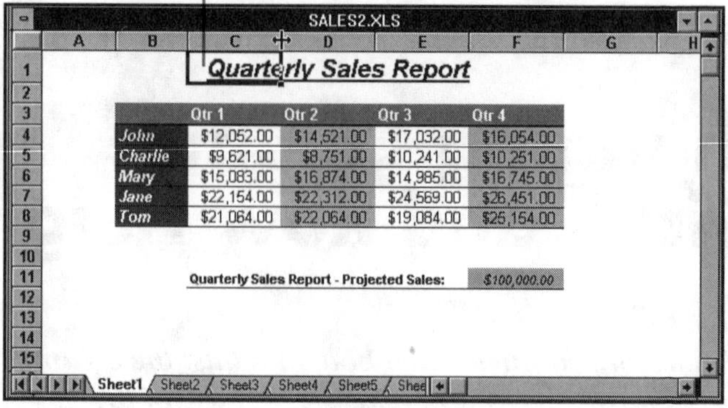

Figure 16.1 The mouse pointer changes when you move it over a border in the row or column heading.

Custom-Fit Cells To quickly make a column as wide as its widest entry, double-click on the right border of the column heading. To make a row as tall as its tallest entry, double-click on the bottom border of the row heading. To change more than one column or row at a time, drag over the desired row or column headings and then double-click on the bottommost or rightmost heading border.

Using the Format Menu

The Format menu contains the commands you need to change the column width and row height of selected rows and columns. Here's how you use the Format menu to change the column width:

1. Select the column(s) whose width you want to change. To change the width of a single column, select any cell in that column.

2. Pull down the Format menu, select Column, and select Width. The Column Width dialog box appears, as shown in Figure 16.2.

3. Type the number of characters you would like as the width. The standard width shown is based on the current default font.

4. Click on OK, or press Enter.

Figure 16.2 Changing the column width.

AutoFit Column Width To make selected columns as wide as their widest entries, select the columns, open the Format menu, select Column, and select AutoFit Selection.

By default, Excel makes a row a bit taller than the tallest text in the row. For example, if the tallest text is 10 points tall, Excel makes the row 12.75 points tall. To use the Format menu to change the row height:

1. Select the row(s) whose height you want to change. To change the height of a single row, select any cell in that row.

2. Pull down the Format menu, select Row and then Height. The Row Height dialog box appears, as shown in Figure 16.3.

3. Type the desired height in points.

4. Click on OK, or press Enter.

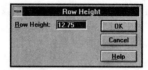

Figure 16.3 Changing the row height.

> **Auto Height** To make selected rows as tall as their tallest entries, select the rows, open the Format menu, select Row, and select AutoFit.

In this lesson, you learned how to change the row height and column width. In the next lesson, you will learn how to use styles (collections of format settings).

Lesson 17

Formatting with Styles

In this lesson, you'll learn how to apply several formatting effects by applying a single style to selected cells.

What Is a Style?

In Lessons 13 through 15, you enhanced a spreadsheet by applying various formats to cells. Styles allow you to apply several formats to a selected cell or cell block by assigning a named style.

> **What's a Style?** A style is a group of cell formatting options that you can apply to a cell or cell block. If you change the style's definition later, that change affects the formatting of all cells formatted with that style.

Each style contains specifications for one or more of the following options:

- **Number Format** controls the appearance of values, such as dollar values and dates.

- **Font** specifies the type style, type size, and any attributes for text contained in the cell.

- **Alignment** specifies general, left, right, or center alignment.

- **Border** specifies the border placement and line style options for the cell.

- **Patterns** adds specified shading to the cell.

- **Protection** allows you to protect or unprotect a cell. However, if you protect a cell or range of cells, the cells are not locked until you protect a worksheet as well by selecting **Tools Protection Protect** Sheet.

Excel has six precreated styles:

Normal   The default style. Number is set to 0, Font to Arial, Size to 10-point, Alignment of numbers is right, and Alignment of text is left, No Border, No Pattern, and Protection is set to locked.

Comma   Number is set to #,##0.00.

Comma (0)   Number is set to #,##0.

Currency   Number is set to $#,##0.00_); (Red) ($#,##0.00).

Currency (0)   Number is set to $#,##0); (Red) ($#,##0).

Percent   Number is set to 0%.

Style Buttons   You can apply most of Excel's existing styles by selecting the cell or cell range and then clicking on the appropriate button in the Formatting toolbar. For example, to set the currency format, select the cells, and then click on the Currency Style button (the button with the dollar sign on it).

Applying Existing Styles

To apply an existing style to a cell or range, perform the following steps:

1. Select the cell or range.

2. Open the Format menu, and select Style. The Style dialog box appears, as shown in Figure 17.1.

3. Click on the down arrow to the right of the Style Name list box, and select the style you want to use.

4. Click on OK or press Enter. The style is applied to the selected cell or range.

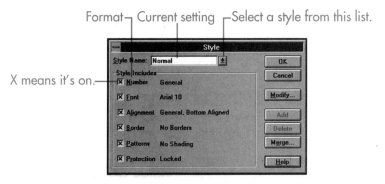

Figure 17.1 Use the Style dialog box to apply styles to cells.

Toolbar Style List Instead of separate Style buttons for each of its existing styles, Excel 4.0 had a style drop-down list in the toolbar. If you miss that list, you can add it back to the toolbar. Choose View Toolbars Customize. Click on the Formatting category, and then drag the Style box up into one of the toolbars. While the Customize dialog box is displayed, you can drag the Style buttons off the toolbar to make room for the Style list.

Creating Styles

To save time, save your favorite formatting combinations as styles. You can create your own styles in various ways:

- Define the style: Create a style, and then assign one or more formatting attributes to it.

- Define by example: Select a cell that contains the formatting you want to use, and then create a style.

- Copy a format: Select a cell in another work book that contains the formatting you want to use, and then merge it with the styles used in the current workbook.

To define a style, perform the following steps:

1. Open the Format menu, and choose Style. The Style dialog box appears.

2. Type a name for the style in the Style Name list box, and click on the Add button. The style is added to the list, and you can now modify it.

3. Remove the **X** from any check box whose attribute you do not want to include in the style. (See Figure 17.2.)

4. To change any of the format settings for the at- tributes in the list, click on the Modify button. Excel displays the Format Cells dialog box.

5. Click on the tab for the format attribute whose settings you want to change, and enter your prefer- ences.

6. Repeat step 5 for each attribute whose settings you want to change.

7. Click on OK, or press Enter. You are returned to the Style dialog box.

8. Click on OK, or press Enter. The Style is created and saved.

Type a name for the new style.

Click on Modify to change the format settings.

Turn a format attribute on or off.

Figure 17.2 Defining a new style.

Modifying a Style Later If you apply a style to one or more cells and then modify the style later, any changes you enter will immediately be applied to all cells you formatted with that style.

To create a new style by example:

1. Select a cell whose formatting you want to use.

2. Open the Format menu, and choose Style.

3. Type a name for the style in the Style Name box.

4. Click on the Add button. The named style is added to the Style Name list box.

5. Click on OK, or press Enter.

To copy existing styles from another workbook:

1. Open both workbooks.

2. Switch to the workbook you want to copy the styles to.

3. Open the Format menu, and choose Style.

4. Click on the Merge button.

5. Select the name of the worksheet to copy from.

6. Click on OK, or press Enter to close the Merge dialog box. If the dialog box asks, "Merge styles that have the same names?" click on Yes.

7. Click on OK, or press Enter.

In this lesson, you learned how to create and apply styles. In the next lesson, you will learn how to create charts.

Lesson 18

Creating Charts

In this lesson, you will learn to create charts (graphs) to represent your workbook data as a picture.

Charting with Excel

With Excel, you can create various types of charts. Some common chart types are shown in Figure 18.1. The chart type you choose depends on your data and on how you want to present that data. These are the major chart types and their purposes:

Pie   Use this chart to show the relationship between parts of a whole.

Bar   Use this chart to compare values at a given point in time.

Column   Similar to the Bar chart; use this chart to emphasize the difference between items.

Line   Use this chart to emphasize trends and the change of values over time.

Area   Similar to the Line chart; use this chart to emphasize the amount of change in values.

Most of these basic chart types also come in 3-dimensional varieties. In addition to looking more professional than the standard flat charts, 3-D charts can often help your audience distinguish between different sets of data.

Bar chart   Pie chart   Column chart

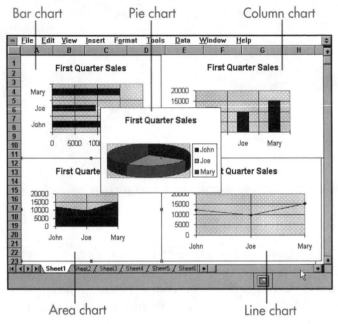

Area chart   Line chart

Figure 18.1   Commonly used Excel chart types.

Embedded Charts   A chart that is placed on
the same worksheet that contains the data used
to create the chart. Embedded charts are useful
for showing the actual data and its graphic
representation side-by-side.

Charting Terminology

Before you start creating charts, familiarize yourself with the
following terminology:

Data Series   A collection of related data, such as the
monthly sales for a single division. A data series is
usually a single row or column on the worksheet.

Axis   One side of a chart. In a two-dimensional chart, there is an X-axis (horizontal) and a Y-axis (vertical). In a three-dimensional chart, the Z-axis represents the vertical plane, and the X-axis (distance) and Y-axis (width) represent the two sides on the floor of the chart.

Legend   Defines the separate elements of a chart. For example, the legend for a pie chart will show what each piece of the pie represents.

Creating a Chart

You can create charts as part of a worksheet (an embedded chart) or as a separate chart worksheet. If you create an embedded chart, it will print side-by-side with your worksheet data. If you create a chart on a chart worksheet, you can print it separately. Both types of charts are linked to the worksheet data that they represent, so when you change the data, the chart is automatically updated.

Creating an Embedded Chart

The ChartWizard button in the Standard toolbar allows you to create a graph frame on a worksheet. To use the ChartWizard, take the following steps:

1. Select the data you want to chart. If you typed names or other labels (for example, Qtr 1, Qtr 2, and so on) and you want them included in the chart, make sure you select them.

2. Click on the ChartWizard button in the Standard toolbar (see Figure 18.2).

3. Move the mouse pointer where you want the upper left corner of the chart to appear.

4. Hold down the mouse button, and drag to define the size and dimensions of the chart. To create a square graph, hold down the Shift key as you drag. If you want your chart to exactly fit the borders of the cells it occupies, hold down the Alt key as you drag.

5. Release the mouse button. The ChartWizard Step 1 of 5 dialog box appears, asking if the selected range is correct. You can correct the range by typing a new range or by dragging the dialog box title bar out of the way, and dragging over the cells you want to chart.

6. Click on the Next button. The ChartWizard Step 2 of 5 dialog box appears, as shown in Figure 18.2, asking you to select a chart type.

Chart types   ChartWizard button

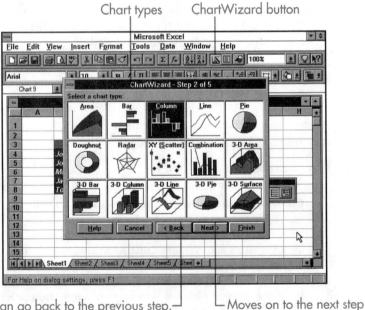

You can go back to the previous step.—   └—Moves on to the next step

Figure 18.2 ChartWizard asks you to choose the chart type you want.

7. Select a chart type, and click on the Next button. The ChartWizard Step 3 of 5 dialog box appears, asking you to select a chart format (a variation on the selected chart type).

8. Select a format for the chosen chart type, and click on the Next button. The ChartWizard Step 4 of 5 dialog box appears, as shown in Figure 18.3. (Your dialog box may look different, depending on the chart type you chose.)

9. Choose whether the data series is based on rows or columns, and choose the starting row and column. Click on the Next button. The ChartWizard Step 5 of 5 dialog box appears.

Select whether you want data graphed by rows or columns.

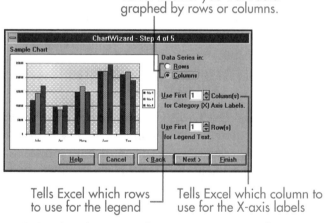

Tells Excel which rows to use for the legend — Tells Excel which column to use for the X-axis labels

Figure 18.3 The ChartWizard prompts you to specify exactly how you want the data charted.

10. If desired, add a legend, title, or axis labels. Click on the Finish button. Your completed chart appears on the current worksheet.

Moving and Resizing a Chart   To move an embedded chart, click anywhere in the chart area and drag it to the new location. To change the size of a chart, select the chart, and then drag one of its handles (the black squares that border the chart). Drag a corner handle to change the height and width, or drag a side handle to change only the width.

Creating a Chart on a Separate Worksheet

If you don't want your chart to appear on the same page as your worksheet data, you can create the chart on a separate worksheet. To create a chart in this way, select the data you want to chart, and then open the Insert menu, choose Chart, and choose As New Sheet. Excel inserts a separate chart worksheet (named Chart 1) to the left of the current worksheet and starts the ChartWizard. Perform the same steps given in the previous section for creating a chart with the ChartWizard.

Using the Chart Toolbar

You can use the Chart toolbar to create a chart, or to change an existing chart, as shown in Figure 18.4. If the Chart toolbar is not displayed, you can turn it on by choosing View Toolbars, placing an **X** in the Chart check box and clicking on OK.

Select a chart type from this list.   Runs the ChartWizard
to edit a selected chart
or make a new one

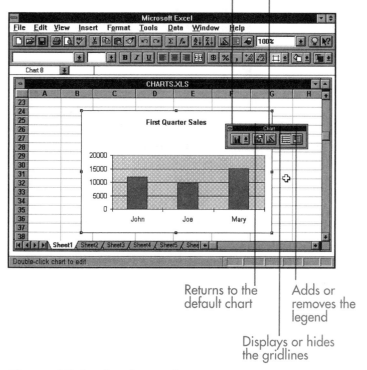

Returns to the   Adds or
default chart   removes the
                      legend

Displays or hides
the gridlines

Figure 18.4   The Chart toolbar.

Still Not Satisfied?   If you need to make
changes to your chart, select the chart, and then
click on the ChartWizard tool to redefine the data
area and make other changes.

Saving Charts

The charts you create are part of the current workbook. To save a chart, simply save the workbook that contains the chart. For more details, refer to Lesson 4, "Working with Workbook Files."

Printing a Chart

If a chart is an embedded chart, it will print when you print the worksheet that contains the chart. If you created a chart on a separate worksheet, you can print the chart separately by printing only the chart worksheet. For more information about printing, refer to Lesson 12, "Printing Your Workbook."

In this lesson, you learned about the different chart types and how to create them. You also learned how to save and print charts. In the next lesson, you will learn how to enhance your charts.

Lesson

Enhancing Charts

In this lesson, you will learn how to enhance your charts to display data more clearly and more attractively.

What Can You Add to a Chart?

You can format existing elements and add elements to a chart to enhance it. Following is a list of some of the more common enhancements:

Fonts   Specify a type style, size, and attributes for the text used in the chart.

Colors   Change the color of text or of the lines, bars, and pie slices that are used to represent data.

Titles and Labels   Add a title to the chart or add labels for any of the axes.

Axes   Display or hide the lines used for the X and Y axes.

Text Boxes   Add explanatory text or other text in a separate box.

Borders and Shading   Add a border around a chart or add background shading.

Text Boxes and Lines Text boxes and lines are available both in charts and in worksheets. Refer to Lesson 20 for details about adding lines and other shapes to charts and worksheets.

Opening a Chart Window

Before you can add enhancements to a chart, you have to open the chart in its own window. To open a chart window for an embedded chart, double-click on the chart to display it in a frame. If the chart is on a separate worksheet, click on its tab to display it in a window. See Figure 19.1. The frame and window serve the same purpose; they just look different.

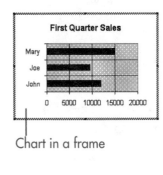

Chart in a frame

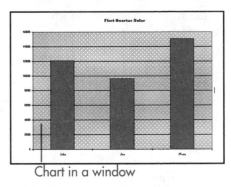

Chart in a window

Figure 19.1 Before you add enhancements, you must display the chart in a window.

Before you start adding enhancements to a chart, you should understand that a chart is made up of several objects. By clicking on an object, you make it active, and handles appear around it, as shown in Figure 19.2. You can then move or resize the object or change its appearance, by doing any of the following:

- Double-click on an object to display a dialog box that lets you change the object's appearance. For example, if you double-click on a column in a column chart, you can change its color.

- Right-click on the object and then select the desired formatting option from the shortcut menu.

- Select the object, and then select an option from the Insert or Format menu. The Insert menu lets you add objects to a chart, including a legend, data labels, and a chart title.

The following sections tell you how to add some more commonly used enhancements to a chart.

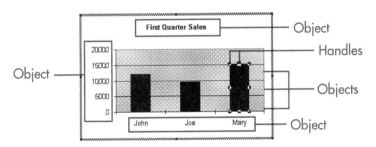

Figure 19.2 Each chart consists of several individual objects.

Adding Titles

You can add various titles to a chart to help indicate what the chart is all about. You can add a chart title that appears at the top of the chart, and you can add axis titles that appear along the X and Y axes. Here's how you do it:

1. Make sure the chart is displayed in a chart window.

2. Right-click on the chart, and choose Insert Titles, or open the Insert menu, and choose Titles.

3. Click on each title type you want to add, to put an **X** in their check boxes.

4. Click on the OK button. Excel returns you to the chart window and inserts text boxes for each title, as shown in Figure 19.3.

5. Click on a text box to select it, click inside the text box, and then edit the text as desired.

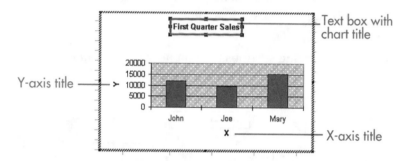

Figure 19.3 Excel inserts text boxes for each specified title.

> **More Text** If you want to add text that is not a chart title or axis title, use the Text Box button in the Standard toolbar (just to the right of the ChartWizard button). Click on the button, and then drag the mouse pointer to create the text box. When you release the mouse button, an insertion point appears inside the text box. Type your text. You can use this same technique to add text to your worksheets as well.

Formatting Text on a Chart

Any text you add to a chart is added inside a text box. (You'll learn how to format text that was lifted from the worksheet data in the next section.) To format text you added, do this:

1. Right-click on the text that you want to format. A text box appears around the text, and a shortcut menu appears.

2. Select the Format option. The Format option differs depending on the object. If you right-click on the chart title, the option reads Format Chart Title.

3. Enter your preferences in the Format dialog box. This dialog box typically contains tabs for changing the font, adding borders and shading to the text box, and changing the alignment of text in the box, but you may get only the Font tab.

4. Click on OK when you are done.

Formatting Text You Did Not Add
Charts may contain some text that was obtained from the worksheet data. A quick way to format this text is to right-click on the chart (not on any specific object), and choose Format Chart Area. Click on the Font tab, enter your preferences, and click on OK.

Formatting the Axes

You can enhance the X and Y axes in a number of ways, including changing the font of the text, scaling the axes, and changing the number format. Here's how you do it:

1. Right-click on the axis you want to format, and choose Format Axis, or click on the axis, open the Format menu, and choose Selected Axis. The Format Axis dialog box appears, as shown in Figure 19.4.

2. Enter your preferences in the dialog box.

3. Click on OK, or press Enter.

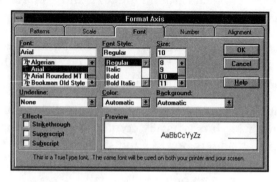

Figure 19.4 The Format Axis dialog box lets you change the look of the axis and its text.

Enhancing the Chart Frame

You can change the overall look of a chart by adding a border or shading. You can do this when the chart is displayed in a window, or when it appears in a worksheet. Here's what you do if the chart is displayed in its own window:

1. Click on the chart anywhere outside a specific chart object. Handles appear around the entire chart.

2. Open the Format menu and choose Selected Chart Area, or right-click on the chart and choose Format Chart Area. The Format Chart Area dialog box appears.

3. Click on the Patterns tab, enter your preferences, and then click on the OK button.

If the chart is not in a separate window, click on the chart, open the Format menu, and choose Object, or right-click on the chart and choose Format Object. The Format Object dialog box appears. Enter your preferences, and then click on OK.

Selecting a Chart Design with AutoFormat

Excel 5 comes with several predesigned chart formats that you can apply to your chart. You simply select the design, and Excel reformats your chart, giving it a professional look. Here's how to use AutoFormat to select a chart design:

1. Make sure the chart is displayed in a separate chart window.

2. Open the Format menu, and choose AutoFormat. The AutoFormat dialog box appears, as shown in Figure 19.5.

3. From the Galleries list, choose a chart type. In the Formats list, Excel shows the available formats for the selected chart type.

4. Select the desired chart type from the Formats list.

5. Click on the OK button. Excel reformats the chart, using the selected format.

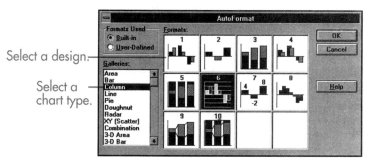

Figure 19.5 Select a chart design from the AutoFormat dialog box.

Make Your Own Formats   You can create
your own chart designs for AutoFormat. Display
the chart you want to use in a separate window.
Open the Format menu, and choose AutoFormat.
Click on User-Defined and then click on the Customize
button. Excel displays the current graph and lets you add
it to AutoFormat. Click on the Add button, type a name
and description of your chart format, click on OK, and
then click on the Close button.

Changing the Look of 3-D Charts

3-D charts are commonly used to illustrate volume. In order
to make the various 3-Dimensional elements stand out, you
may want to tilt the chart or rotate it. Here's how you do it:

1. Make sure the 3-D chart you want to change is
    displayed in its own window.

2. Open the Format menu and choose 3-D View, or
    right-click on the chart and choose 3-D View. The
    Format 3-D View dialog box appears, as shown in
    Figure 19.6. As you make changes, they are re-
    flected in the wire-frame picture in the middle of
    the 3-D View dialog box.

3. To change the elevation (height from which the
    chart is seen), click on the up or down elevation
    controls, or type a number in the Elevation box.

4. To change the rotation (rotation around the Z-axis),
    click on the left or right rotation controls, or type a
    number in the Rotation box.

5. To change the perspective (perceived depth), click
    on the up or down perspective controls, or type a
    number in the Perspective box.

6. To see the proposed changes applied to the actual
    chart, click on the Apply button.

7. When you are done making changes, click on OK,
    or press Enter.

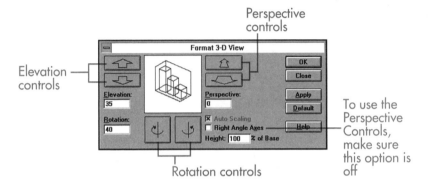

Figure 19.6 Changing the 3-D view.

In this lesson, you learned how to improve the appearance of your chart. In the next lesson, you will learn how to
use Excel's drawing tools to enhance the appearance of
worksheets and charts.

Lesson

20

Adding Graphics to Charts and Workbooks

In this lesson, you will learn how to add graphic objects to your charts and worksheets.

Working with Graphic Objects

Excel comes with several tools that allow you to add pictures to your workbooks and charts. You can add a picture created in another program, you can add clip art, or you can draw your own pictures using the Drawing toolbar.

> **Graphic Object** A graphic object is anything in your worksheet that isn't data. Graphic objects include things you can draw (such as ovals and rectangles), text boxes, charts, and clip art.

Inserting Pictures

If you have a collection of clip art or pictures that you created and saved using a graphics program or scanner, you can insert those pictures on a worksheet or in a chart. To insert a picture, do this:

1. Select the cell where you want the upper left corner of the picture placed. (To insert the picture in a chart, double-click on the chart to display it in a separate window.)

2. Open the Insert menu, and choose Picture. The Picture dialog box appears, as shown in Figure 20.1.

3. Change to the drive and directory that contains your clip art or graphics files. A list of graphics files appears in the File Name list.

4. Select the name of the graphics file you want to insert, and click on the OK button. Excel imports the picture.

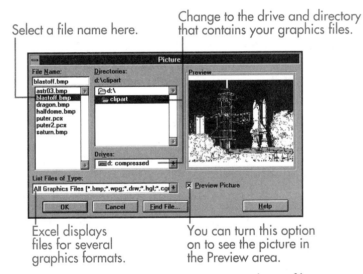

Select a file name here.

Change to the drive and directory that contains your graphics files.

Excel displays files for several graphics formats.

You can turn this option on to see the picture in the Preview area.

Figure 20.1 You can insert a picture or a clip art file.

You can move the picture by dragging it. To resize the picture, drag one of its handles. Drag a corner handle to change both the width and height. Drag a side handle to change only the width, or drag a top or bottom handle to change only the height.

Copy and Paste Pictures   Another way to insert a picture is to copy it from one program and then paste it in Excel. First, display the picture in the program you used to create it, and use the Edit Copy command in that program to copy it to the Windows Clipboard. Change back to Excel, and use the Edit Paste command to paste the picture from the Clipboard into your workbook or graph.

Inserting Other Objects

In addition to pictures, you can insert objects created in other programs. For example, you can insert a sound recording (if you have a sound board that has a microphone attached) or WordArt objects (if you have Microsoft Publisher or Word for Windows). When you choose to insert an object, Excel runs the required program and lets you create the object. When you quit the other program, the object is inserted on the current chart or worksheet. Here's what you do:

1. Select the cell where you want the upper left corner of the picture placed. (To insert the picture in a chart, double-click on the chart to display it in a separate window.)

2. Open the Insert menu, and choose Object. The Object dialog box appears, as shown in Figure 20.2.

3. Make sure the Create New tab is up front. The Create New tab lets you run another program and create the object. Create from File allows you to insert an object that you have already created and saved.

4. Select the program you need to run to create the object from the Object Type list.

5. Click on the OK button. Excel runs the selected program.

6. Use the program as you normally would to create the object. When you are done, save the object, and exit the program as you usually do. When you exit, a dialog box appears asking if you want to update the link before exiting.

7. Choose Yes.

Create from File The Create from File tab is sort of like using **I**nsert **P**icture; both commands insert an object without running a program.

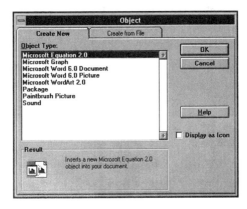

Figure 20.2 Select the program you need to create the object.

Drawing Your Own Pictures

If you don't have a drawing program, or you don't want to use it to create a separate file, you can use Excel's Drawing toolbar to create a picture or add simple lines and shapes to a chart or workbook. To turn on the Drawing toolbar, choose View Toolbars, click on Drawing, and click on OK. The Drawing toolbar appears on-screen, as shown in Figure 20.3.

Drawing tools

Tools for working
with drawn objects

Figure 20.3   The Drawing toolbar lets you add shapes and
lines to your workbook.

Drawing Objects

To draw an object, you select the tool for the line or shape
you want to use and then drag the shape on the screen.
Here's the step-by-step procedure:

1. Click on the desired tool on the Drawing toolbar.
   Your mouse will change to a cross-hair pointer.

2. Move the cross-hair pointer to the upper left corner
   of where you would like to draw the object.

3. Hold down the mouse button, and drag the pointer
   until the object is the size and shape you want. See
   Figure 20.4.

4. Release the mouse button.

Tips for Working with Objects

Following is a list of additional drawing tips that can save you
some time and reduce frustration:

- To draw several objects of the same shape, double-
  click on the tool, and then use the mouse to create
  as many of those shapes as you like.

- To draw a uniform object (a perfect circle or
  square), hold down the Shift key while dragging.

- To select an object, click on it.

- To delete an object, select it, and press Del.

- To move an object, select it, and drag one of its lines.

- To resize or reshape an object, select it, and drag one of its handles. If you used one of the Freeform tools or the Freehand tool to draw an irregularly shaped object, you must click on the Reshape button to reshape the object.

- To copy an object, hold down the Ctrl key while dragging it.

- To quickly change the look of an object, right-click on it, and select the desired option from the short-cut menu.

Drawing tools are the first row of buttons.

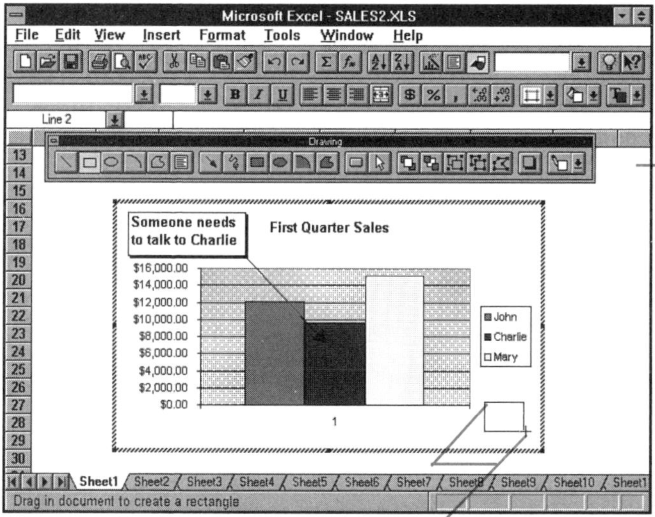

Drag from one corner to the opposite corner.

Figure 20.4 Drawing an object on a chart.

Working with Layers of Objects

As you place objects on-screen, they may start to overlap, making it difficult or impossible to select the objects in the lower layer. To reveal or work with items in the lower layers, you may have to use the Bring To Front and Send To Back buttons shown in Figure 20.5.

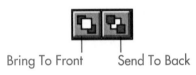

Bring To Front   Send To Back

Figure 20.5   Use these buttons to relayer overlapping objects.

Grouping and Ungrouping Objects

Each object you draw acts as an individual object. However, sometimes you'll want two or more objects to act as a group. For example, you may want to make the lines of several objects the same thickness, or move the objects together. To select more than one object, you have two options:

Option 1: Hold down the Shift key while clicking on each object you want to include in the group.

Option 2: Click on the Drawing Selection button (the button with the mouse pointer on it) in the Drawing toolbar, and then use the mouse to drag a selection box around the items you want included in the group.

However you do it, handles appear around each object, showing you that it is selected. If you want two or more objects to always be treated as a group, select the objects, and then click on the Group Objects button. To ungroup the objects later, click on the Ungroup Objects button. See Figure 20.6.

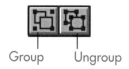

Group   Ungroup

Figure 20.6   Excel lets you group or ungroup objects.

Changing the Appearance of an Object

Objects typically are made up of a thin, black line with white or gray shading inside it. If you want to add color to an object, or change its line thickness or color, you must format the object. There are three ways to format an object:

- Right-click on the object, and choose Format Object.

- Click on the object, open the Format menu, and choose Selected Object, or press Ctrl+1.

- Double-click on the object.

Any way you do it, the Format Object dialog box appears. Enter your preferences, and then click on the OK button.

In this lesson, you learned how to add graphic objects and other objects to your worksheets and charts. In the next lesson, you will learn how to turn your worksheet data into a database.

Lesson

Creating a Database

In this lesson, you will learn how to create your own database.

Database Basics

A *database* is a tool used for storing, organizing, and retrieving information. For example, if you want to save the names and addresses of all the people on your holiday card list, you can create a database for storing the following information for each person: first name, last name, street number, and so on. Each piece of information is entered into a separate *field*. All of the fields for one person on the list make a *record*. In Excel, a cell is a field, and a row of field entries makes a record. Figure 21.1 shows a database and its component parts.

> **Database or Data List?** Excel has simplified the database operations by treating the database as a simple *list* of data. This data acts as any other worksheet data, until you select a command from the **Data** menu. Then, Excel recognizes the list as a database.

You must observe the following rules when you enter information into your database:

- *Field Names:* You must enter field names in the first row of the database; for example, type **First Name** for first name, and **Last Name** for the last name. Do NOT skip a row between the field names row and the first record.

- *Records:* Each record must be in a separate row, with no empty rows between records. The cells in a given column must contain information of the same type. For example, if you have a ZIP CODE column, all cells in that column must contain a ZIP code. You can create a calculated field; one that uses information from another field of the same record and produces a result. (To do so, enter a formula, as explained in Lesson 10.)

Field names are used as column headings.

	A	B	C	D	E	F	G
1	Record #	First Name	Last Name	Address	City	State	ZIP Code
2	1	William	Kennedy	5567 Bluehill Circle	Indianapolis	IN	46224
3	2	Marion	Kraft	1313 Mockingbird Lane	Los Angeles	CA	77856
4	3	Mary	Abolt	8517 Grandview Avenue	San Diego	CA	77987
5	4	Joseph	Fugal	2764 W. 56th Place	Chicago	IL	60678
6	5	Gregg	Lawrence	5889 N. Bringshire Blvd.	Boston	MA	56784
7	6	Lisa	Kasdan	8976 Westhaven Drive	Orlando	FL	86329
8	7	Nicholas	Capetti	1345 W. Bilford Ave.	New Orleans	LA	12936
9	8	Allison	Milton	32718 S. Visionary Drive	Phoenix	AZ	97612
10	9	Barry	Strong	908 N. 9th Street	Chicago	IL	60643
11	10	Chuck	Burger	6754 W. Lakeview Drive	Boston	MA	56784
12	11	Carey	Bistro	987 N. Cumbersome Lane	Detroit	MI	86687
13	12	Marie	Gabel	8764 N. Demetrius Blvd.	Miami	FL	88330
14	13	Adrienne	Bullow	5643 N. Gaylord Ave.	Philadelphia	PA	27639
15	14	John	Kramden	5401 N. Bandy	Pittsburgh	PA	27546
16	15	Mitch	Kroll	674 E. Cooperton Drive	Seattle	WA	14238

ADDRESS2.XLS

Sheet1 / Sheet2 / Sheet3 / Sheet4 / Sheet5 / Sheet

Each row is a record.　　　Each cell contains a single field entry.

Figure 21.1　The parts of a database.

Record Numbering　It is a good idea to add a column that numbers the records. If the records are sorted incorrectly, you can use the numbered column to restore the records to their original order.

Planning a Database

Before you create a database, you should ask yourself a few
questions:

- What fields make up an individual record? If you are
  creating the database to take the place of an existing form (a Rolodex card, information sheet, or
  address list), use that form to determine which
  fields you need.

- What is the most often referenced field in the
  database? (This field should be placed in the first
  column.)

- What is the longest entry in each column? (Use this
  information to set the column widths. Otherwise,
  you can make your entries and then use Format
  Column AutoFit Selection to have Excel adjust the
  column widths.)

Creating a Database

To create a database, enter data into the cells as you would
enter data on any worksheet. As you enter data, follow these
guidelines:

- You must enter field names in the top row of the
  database.

- Type field entries into each cell in a single row to
  create a record. (You can leave a field blank, but
  you may run into problems later when you sort the
  database.)

- Do NOT leave an empty row between the field
  names and the records or between any records.

- If you want to enter street numbers with the street
  names, start the entry with an apostrophe so that
  Excel interprets the entry as text instead of as a
  value.

- Keep the records on one worksheet. You cannot have a database that spans several worksheets.

Forget Someone?   To add records to a defined database, either add the rows above the last row in the database, or use the Data Form dialog box.

In the previous version of Excel (Excel 4.0 and earlier), you had to enter a command to transform the data you type into a database. In Excel 5, this step is unnecessary. Excel 5 treats the data you typed as a *list*. Whenever you select a database command from the **Data** menu, Excel automatically treats the list as a database.

Using Data Forms to Add, Edit, or Delete Records

Data forms are like index cards; there is one data form for each record in the database, as shown in Figure 21.2. You may find it easier to flip through these data form "cards" and edit entries rather than editing them as worksheet data. To display a data form, open the Data menu, and select Form.

To flip from one form to the next or previous form, use the scroll bar, or the ↑ or ↓ key. To edit an entry in a record, tab to the text box that contains the entry, and type your correction. Press Enter when you're done.

Come Back!   To restore data changed in a field before you press Enter, select the Restore button.

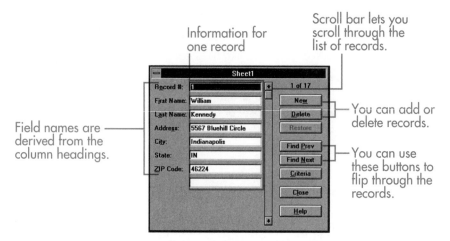

Figure 21.2 The Data Form dialog box.

You can also use the Data Form dialog box to add records to the database:

1. Select the New button.

2. Type an entry into each of the text boxes.

3. Click on OK, or press Enter.

To delete a record:

1. Select the record you want to change by selecting the Find Prev or Find Next buttons, or by using the scroll bars or up and down arrow keys to move through the database.

2. Select Delete.

3. Click on OK, or press Enter.

When you are done with the Data Form dialog box, click on the Close button.

In this lesson, you learned how to create a database. In the next lesson, you will learn how to sort the database and find individual records.

22

Finding and Sorting Data in a Database

In this lesson, you will learn how to sort a database and how to find individual records.

Finding Data with a Data Form

To find records in a database, you must specify the individual criteria (the specific information or range of information you want to find). You could type something specific like Red under the Color field of the form, or something that must be evaluated, like <1000 (less than 1000) in the Sales field. Table 22.1 shows the operators that you can use for comparison:

Table 22.1 Excel's Comparison Operators

Operator	Meaning
=	Equal to
>	Greater than
<	Less than
>=	Greater than or equal to
<=	Less than or equal to
<>	Not equal to

You can also use the following wild cards when specifying criteria:

?   Represents a single character

*   Represents multiple characters

For example, in the Name field, type M* to find everyone whose name begins with an *M*. To find everyone whose three-digit department code has *10* as the last two digits, type ?10.

To find individual records in a database:

1.   Pull down the Data menu, and select Form. The Data Form dialog box appears.

2.   Click on the Criteria button; the dialog box shown in Figure 22.1 appears.

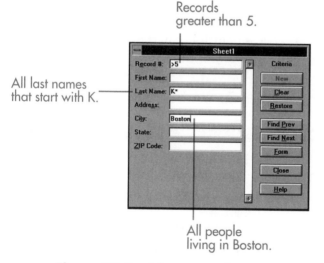

Records greater than 5.

All last names that start with K.

All people living in Boston.

Figure 22.1   Selecting search criteria.

3. Type the criteria you would like to use in the appropriate fields. Use only the fields you want to search. For example, if you want to find all Texans whose last name starts with *B*, you could type TX in the State field and B* in the Last Name field.

4. Click on Form, or press Enter.

5. Select Find Next or Find Prev to locate certain matching records.

6. When you are done reviewing records, select Close.

Sorting Data in a Database

To sort a database, first decide which field to sort on. For example, an address database could be sorted by Name or by City (or it could be sorted by Name within City within State). Each of these sort fields is considered a *key*.

You can use up to three keys when sorting your database. The first key in the above example would be Name, then City, and then State. You can sort your database in ascending or descending order.

Sort Orders   Ascending order is from beginning to end, for example from A to Z or 1 to 10. Descending order is backward, from Z to A or 10 to 1.

For the Record   When you select the database range to sort, include all of the records but not the column headings (field names). If you select the column heading row, it will be sorted along with all the other rows and may not remain at the top.

To sort your database:

1. Select the area to be sorted. To sort the entire data list, select any cell in the list.

2. Pull down the Data menu, and choose Sort. The Sort dialog box appears, as shown in Figure 22.2.

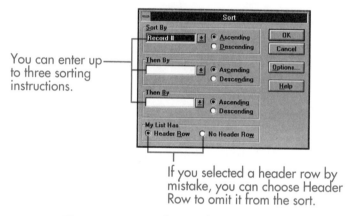

You can enter up to three sorting instructions.

If you selected a header row by mistake, you can choose Header Row to omit it from the sort.

Figure 22.2 Selecting the sort criteria.

3. Use the Sort By drop-down list to select the first field you want to sort on, and click on Ascending or Descending to specify a sort order.

4. To sort on another field, repeat step 3 for the first and second Then By drop-down lists.

5. Click on OK, or press Enter.

Undoing a Sort If the sorting operation does not turn out as planned, you can undo the sort by selecting the Undo Sort command on the Edit menu (or pressing Ctrl+Z). To sort even more safely, you might also consider saving your database file before sorting. That way, if anything goes wrong, you can open your original database file.

Quick Sort   To quickly sort by the first column entries, use the Sort Ascending or Sort Descending buttons on the Standard toolbar.

Narrowing Your List with AutoFilter

Excel 5 offers a new feature called AutoFilter that allows you to easily display only a select group of records in your database. For example, you can display the records for only those people who live in Boston. Here's how you use AutoFilter:

1. Select the entire database, including the row you used for headings.

2. Open the Data menu, select Filter, and select AutoFilter. Excel displays drop-down list arrow buttons inside each cell at the top of your database.

3. Click on the drop-down list button for the field you want to use to filter the list. For example, if you want to display records for those people living in Boston, click on the button in the City cell. A drop-down list appears, as shown in Figure 22.3. This list contains all the entries in the column.

4. Select the entry you want to use to narrow your list. You can use the arrow keys to scroll through the list, or type the first character in the entry's name to quickly move to it. Press Enter, or click on the entry with your mouse. Excel filters the list.

Click on the arrow to
display the drop-down list.

	A	B	C	D	E	F	G
1	Record	First Nam	Last Nam	Address	City	Sta	ZIP Cor
2	7	Nicholas	Capetti	1345 W. Bilford Ave.	(All)	LA	12936
3	13	Adrienne	Bullow	5643 N. Gaylord Ave.	[Custom...]	PA	27639
4	14	John	Kramden	5401 N. Bandy	Boston	PA	27546
5	15	Mitch	Kroll	674 E. Cooperton Drive	Chicago	WA	14238
6	1	William	Kennedy	5567 Bluehill Circle	Detroit	IN	46224
7	18	Joe	Kraynak	5525 West Market Street	Indianapolis	IN	46224
8	17	Kathy	Estrich	8763 W. Cloverdale Ave.	Los Angeles	TX	54812
9	10	Chuck	Burger	6754 W. Lakeview Drive	Miami	MA	56784
10	5	Gregg	Lawrence	5689 N. Bringshire Blvd.	Boston	MA	56784
11	9	Barry	Strong	908 N. 9th Street	Chicago	IL	60643
12	4	Joseph	Fugal	2764 W. 56th Place	Chicago	IL	60678
13	16	Gary	Davell	76490 E. Billview	New York	NY	76453
14	2	Marion	Kraft	1313 Mockingbird Lane	Los Angeles	CA	77656
15	3	Mary	Abolt	8517 Grandview Avenue	San Diego	CA	77987
16	6	Lisa	Kasdan	8976 Westhaven Drive	Orlando	FL	88329

ADDRESS2.XLS

Sheet1 / Sheet2 / Sheet3 / Sheet4 / Sheet5 / Shee

Figure 22.3 AutoFilter lets you narrow your list.

Unfiltering a List To return to the full list,
open the drop-down list again, and choose (All).
You can turn AutoFilter off by selecting **D**ata **F**ilter
AutoFilter.

  In this lesson, you learned how to find individual
records and how to sort and filter your database. In the next
lesson, you will learn how to use the data in your database to
create a report.

Lesson 23

Summarizing and Comparing Data in a Database

In this lesson, you will learn how to summarize data in complex databases to create reports.

Using the PivotTable Wizard

Excel 5.0 has improved its Crosstab ReportWizard, and has renamed it the PivotTable Wizard. This feature allows you to create reports that summarize worksheet data and lay it out in a more meaningful format. For example, suppose you had a database that kept track of your monthly sales, by product and salesperson. You can create a report that summarizes the amount of each product sold each month by each salesperson. You can then quickly rearrange the table to analyze the data in various ways. Figure 23.1 illustrates how a pivot table works.

First Encounters   If this is your first encounter with pivot tables, expect to spend some time working with them. Once you get the hang of the data buttons, it will seem easy to you, but getting the hang of the data buttons takes patience.

You can quickly rearrange data by dragging the field buttons.

Worksheet data list

Totals are for all months January–March.

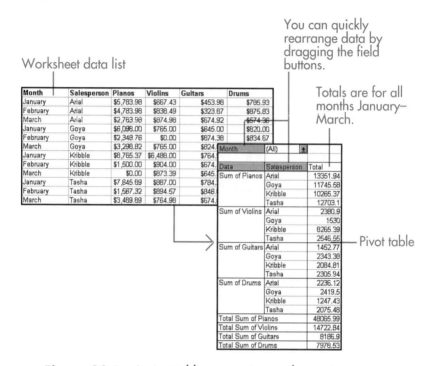

Pivot table

Figure 23.1 A pivot table summarizes and organizes your data.

When you create a pivot table, you must specify four elements:

Pages Pages allow you to create a drop-down list for one of the rows or columns in your worksheet. For example, you can use the Salesperson column to create a drop-down list that contains the names of all your salespeople. Select a salesperson from the list to see how much of each item that person is selling per month.

Rows Cells that form the rows for the report. You can have up to eight rows. For example, these could be *months*.

Columns   Cells that form the column headings for the report. You can have up to eight columns. For example, this could be *salespeople*.

Sum of Value   These are the values you want added for each intersection of a column or row. For example, displaying months in rows and salespeople in columns indicates how much each salesperson sold each month.

Creating a Pivot Table

You create a pivot table by running Excel's PivotTable Wizard, which leads you through the process with a series of dialog boxes. Here's how you use the PivotTable Wizard:

1. Open the Data menu, and select PivotTable. Excel displays the PivotTable Wizard Step 1 of 4 dialog box.

2. Click on the Next button. The PivotTable Wizard Step 2 of 4 dialog box appears, asking you to select the range of cells you want to transform into a pivot table. Excel shows a blinking dotted box that indicates what data it thinks you want to use.

3. Type the cell addresses that define the range, or drag over the desired cells with the mouse pointer.

4. Click on the Next button. The PivotTable Wizard Step 3 of 4 dialog box appears.

5. Drag the buttons on the right where you want the row headings, column headings, or data to appear, as shown in Figure 23.2.

6. Click on the Next button. The PivotTable Wizard
    Step 4 of 4 dialog box appears, asking if you want to
    specify additional preferences and location for the
    pivot table.

7. Enter you preferences, and then click on the Finish
    button. The PivotTable Wizard creates the table
    according to your specifications.

If you did not specify a location for the pivot table in
step 7, the Wizard inserts a worksheet before the current
worksheet and sets the pivot table on the new worksheet. To
see your original data, click on its worksheet tab.

Not Quite What You Expected? When the
PivotTable Wizard is done, it creates a table that
may or may not be exactly what you wanted.
Don't worry. You can rearrange the data simply by
dragging field buttons around on-screen.

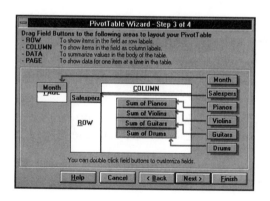

Figure 23.2 Drag the field buttons to specify how you want
the table arranged.

Appendix

Microsoft Windows Primer

Microsoft Windows is an interface program that makes your computer easier to use by enabling you to select menu items and pictures rather than type commands. Before you can take advantage of it, however, you must learn some Windows basics.

Starting Microsoft Windows

To start Windows, do the following:

1. At the DOS prompt, type win.

2. Press Enter.

The Windows title screen appears for a few moments, and then you see a screen like the one in Figure A.1.

What If It Didn't Work? You may have to change to the Windows directory before starting Windows; to do so, type CD \WINDOWS and press Enter. Then, type win and press Enter.

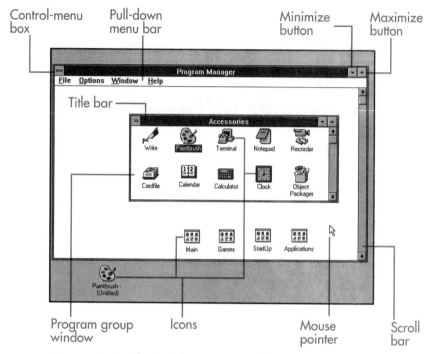

Control-menu box
Pull-down menu bar
Minimize button
Maximize button
Title bar
Program group window
Icons
Mouse pointer
Scroll bar

Figure A.1   The Windows Program Manager.

Parts of a Windows Screen

As shown in Figure A.1, the Windows screen contains several unique elements that you won't see in DOS. Here's a brief summary.

- *Title bar*   Shows the name of the window or program.

- *Program group windows*   Contain program icons that allow you to run programs.

- *Icons*   Graphic representations of programs. To run a program, you select its icon.

- *Minimize and Maximize buttons*   Alter a window's size. The Minimize button shrinks the window to the size of an icon. The Maximize button expands the window to fill the screen. When maximized, a window contains a double-arrow *Restore* button, which returns the window to its original size.

- *Control-menu box*   When selected, pulls down a menu that offers size and location controls for the window.

- *Pull-down menu bar*   Contains a list of the pull-down menus available in the program.

- *Mouse pointer*   If you are using a mouse, the mouse pointer (usually an arrow) appears on-screen. It can be controlled by moving the mouse (discussed later in this appendix).

- *Scroll bars*   If a window contains more information than it can display, you will see a scroll bar. *Scroll arrows* on each end of the scroll bar allow you to scroll slowly. The *scroll box* allows you to scroll more quickly.

Using a Mouse

To work most efficiently in Windows, you should use a mouse. You can press mouse buttons and move the mouse in various ways to change the way it acts:

Point means to move the mouse pointer onto the specified item by moving the mouse. The tip of the mouse pointer must be touching the item.

Click on an item means to move the pointer onto the specified item and press the mouse button once. Unless specified otherwise, use the left mouse button.

Double-click on an item means to move the pointer onto the specified item and press and release the left mouse button twice quickly.

Drag means to move the mouse pointer onto the specified item, hold down the mouse button, and move the mouse while holding down the button.

Figure A.2 shows how to use the mouse to perform common Windows activities, including running applications, and moving and resizing windows.

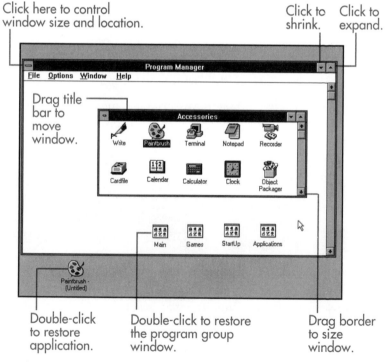

Figure A.2   Use your mouse to control Windows.

Starting a Program

To start a program, simply double-click its icon. If its icon is contained in a program group window that's not open at the moment, open the window first. Follow these steps:

1. If necessary, open the program group window that contains the program you want to run. To open a program group window, double-click on its icon.

2. Double-click on the icon for the program you want to run.

Using Menus

The pull-down menu bar (see Figure A.3) contains various menus from which you can select commands. Each Windows program that you run has a set of pull-down menus; Windows itself has a set, too.

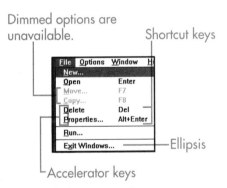

Figure A.3   A pull-down menu lists various commands you can perform.

To open a menu, click on its name on the menu bar. Once a menu is open, you can select a command from it by clicking on the desired command.

Accelerator Keys   Notice that in Figure A.3, some commands are followed by key names such as Enter (for the Open command) or F8 (for the Copy command). These are called *shortcut keys*. You can use these keys to perform the commands without even opening the menu.

Usually, when you select a command, the command is performed immediately. However:

- If the command name is gray (rather than black), the command is unavailable at the moment, and you cannot choose it.

- If the command name is followed by an arrow, selecting the command will cause another menu to appear.

- If the command name is followed by ellipsis (three dots), selecting it will cause a dialog box to appear. You'll learn about dialog boxes in the next section.

Navigating Dialog Boxes

A dialog box is Windows' way of requesting additional information. For example, if you choose Options from the Tools menu in Excel, you'll see the dialog box shown in Figure A.4.

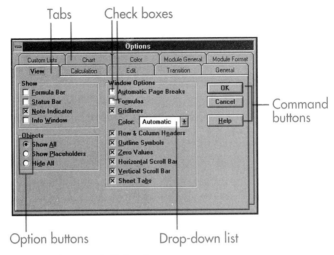

Figure A.4 A typical dialog box.

Each dialog box contains one or more of the following elements:

- **Tabs** are like pages. To switch to a tab page, click on its tab, or press Ctrl+Tab.

- **List boxes** display available choices. To activate a list, click inside the list box. To select an item from the list, click on it.

- **Drop-down lists** are similar to list boxes, but only one item in the list is shown. To see the rest of the items, click on the down arrow to the right of the list box.

- **Text boxes** allow you to type an entry. To activate a text box, click inside it.

- **Check boxes** allow you to select one or more items in a group of options. Click on a check box to activate it.

- **Option buttons** are like check boxes, but you can select only one option button in a group. Selecting one button unselects any option that is already selected.

- **Command buttons** execute (or cancel) the command once you have made your selections in the dialog box. To press a command button, click on it.

Switching Between Windows

Many times, you will have more than one window open at once. Some open windows may be program group windows, while others may be actual programs that are running. To switch among them, you can pull down the Window menu, and choose the window you want to view, or, if a portion of the desired window is visible, click on it.

Controlling a Window

As you saw earlier, you can minimize, maximize, and restore windows. But you can also move them and change their size.

- To move a window, drag its title bar to a different location. (Remember, drag means to hold down the left mouse button while you move the mouse.)

- To resize a window, position the mouse pointer on the border of the window until you see a double-headed arrow; then drag the window border to the desired size.

Index